Lockers, Lunch Lines, Chemistry, and Cliques...

77 Pretty Important Ideas

Lockers, Lunchlines, Chemistry, and Cliques
Cars, Curfews, Parties, and Parents
Camp, Car Washes, Heaven, and Hell
Life, Love, Music, and Money

Lockers, Lunch Lines, Chemistry, and Cliques...

SUSIE SHELLENBERGER
& GREG JOHNSON

BETHANY HOUSE PUBLISHERS
MINNEAPOLIS, MINNESOTA 55438

Published by Bethany House Publishers
A Ministry of Bethany Fellowship International
11400 Hampshire Avenue South
Minneapolis, Minnesota 55438
www.bethanyhouse.com

Printed in the United States of America by
Bethany Press International, Minneapolis, Minnesota 55438

Library of Congress Cataloging-in-Publication Data

Shellenberger, Susie.
    Lockers, lunch lines, chemistry, and cliques : 77 pretty important ideas for
school survival / Susie Shellenberger, Greg Johnson.
        p.   cm. — (77 pretty important ideas for survival)
    Summary: Offers advice on dealing with a variety of common concerns for
high school students, including cheating, taking showers in P.E. class, getting
along with teachers, and more—all from the Christian perspective.

    1. High school students—Handbooks, manuals, etc.—Juvenile literature.
2. High school students—Conduct of life—Handbooks, manuals, etc.—Juvenile
literature. [1. High schools. 2. Schools. 3. Christian life. 4. Conduct of
life.] I. Johnson, Greg. II. Title. III. Series: Shellenberger, Susie. 77 pretty
important ideas for survival.
LB3605.S51153   1994
373.18—dc20   94-49218
ISBN 1-55661-483-7   CIP
                                                                                                  AC

Dedicated to . . .

Jennifer Bergland

who lives and teaches

with enthusiasm, motivation, and integrity.

—Susie Shellenberger

SUSIE SHELLENBERGER is the editor of *Brio* magazine for teen girls (cir. 160,000), published by FOCUS ON THE FAMILY. A graduate of SOUTHERN NAZARENE UNIVERSITY and the UNIVERSITY OF CENTRAL OKLAHOMA, Susie's experience with teens ranges from youth ministry to teaching high school speech and drama. She is the author of nine books, including *There's a Sheep in My Mirror* and *Straight Ahead*.

GREG JOHNSON is the former editor of *Breakaway* magazine for teen boys (cir. 90,000) and the author or co-author of fifteen books, including *If I Could Ask God One Question* and *Daddy's Home*. A graduate of NORTHWEST CHRISTIAN COLLEGE, Greg has been involved with teens for over fifteen years and has worked with YOUTH FOR CHRIST and FOCUS ON THE FAMILY. He and his wife have two sons and make their home in Colorado Springs, where Greg is a literary agent for ALIVE COMMUNICATIONS.

Start the day by letting GOD know you want Him with you.

Some people aren't too awake in the morning, so challenging them to take fifteen to thirty minutes to read their Bible and pray is wasted space. But everyone can say a prayer asking God to guide them, help them make good decisions, treat others the way Jesus would, and honor Him by what they say and do. If you mean it, God will answer.

But if you **CAN** spend a few minutes in the Word or with a devotional book of some sort (and most teens can), by all means, do it. **Getting your mind on the right track** the very first thing of the day **is the best habit** you could ever get into. Satan will do all he can to keep you from it, so you know how important he knows it must be. Find a Christian friend you can team up with and call each other at 7:15 A.M. every day to make sure you'll spend the next fifteen minutes with God. Without a friend to help you along, you'll find it next to impossible to accomplish.

No matter how desperate you are,
DON'T cheat!

Josh was one of the best basketball players in our high school. He was also a Christian and a fun guy. I (Susie) enjoyed being his English teacher. But he was a **terrible** speller. This usually didn't affect him on the court. (After all, he didn't have to know how to **spell** the strategy, just how to use it!)

But the semester was drawing to a close, and Josh's English grades were on a downward spiral. In fact, he was in danger of the "No Pass/No Play" penalty. **I guess that's why he figured it would be okay to cheat.**

It wasn't too hard to catch him. He'd been failing spelling tests all year long. When he suddenly started acing words like "Yoknapatawpha" (where American author William Faulkner lived), it was pretty obvious something was up his sleeve . . . *literally.* I confiscated the microscopic cheat-sheet from inside his wristwatch!

So I pulled him out in the hall and sat down on the floor with him. When he caught my eye, I began. "You've been cheating, right?"

His shoulders sagged and he looked away. "Now—out here in the hall—with you, I know it was wrong. But you know what? **It seemed okay at the time."**

"Josh," I said, "I'm not as concerned about your grades as I am about your relationship with Christ. Whatever made you think you could compromise?"

While the rest of my class headed to the library, Josh and I sat on a dirty-tiled floor and talked about forgiveness, integrity, and rationalizing.

"I just wanted to play basketball. But I didn't mean to do something wrong just to keep playing. Or maybe I did. I don't know. I'm all confused."

"Josh, is it right for an adult to cheat on income taxes?"

"No, of course not."

"And would it ever be right for me to show up at school at 7:55, but sign in at 7:30?"

"No—you'd be lying."

"Well, then," I said, "is it ever right for someone to cheat? To take a grade he didn't honestly earn?"

"Nope."

I rearranged some of the dirt on the floor while he smashed a bug. Then he continued. "**But everyone cheats.** You know they do."

"Yeah. I know. But guess what, Josh?"

He expected me to continue, but I waited and made him say:

"What?"

"Everyone's not living a godly life. **And everyone's not going to heaven.** You're a Christian."

"Yeah, but I'm still human."

"Me, too. And we **ALL** blow it. That's why God's forgiveness comes in handy. But guess what, Josh?"

He thought I'd just keep going, but I waited again and made him say:

"What?"

"God expects us to live above what everyone else is doing. That's what being *in* the world but not being *of* it is all about."

Then I stopped. Clayton Davis was strolling down the hall, and I wondered what excuse he'd used to con Mrs. Brown into letting him out of class. He was **always** trying to get out of class: The library. The drinking fountain.

The guidance counselor. The home-ec room to check his souffle. The bathroom. I was halfway off the floor to demand a hall pass when Josh voiced his thoughts.

"I know how you feel about cheating. And I know it was wrong for me to cheat. I guess I just got carried away. I mean basketball is really important to me. But you know what, Miss Shellenberger?"

I expected him to keep going, but he waited and made me say: "What?" **"My relationship with God is more important.** Thanks for reminding me."

"Yeah, well . . . get to the library with the rest of the class. You're gonna need all the reference books you can get your hands on if you expect to make up your bogus test scores with enough extra-credit work to get you out of this 'No Pass/No Play' scenario."

"Really? You're giving me extra-credit work? I can play! Thanks. Thanks. I mean, **really** thanks. I love having a Christian teacher. Who says public schools are jungles?"

"You've got thirty seconds to get to the library, or you'll have detention for a week."

● - ● - ●

Even though Josh knew cheating was wrong, he found it easy to rationalize because he believed it was for a good cause. In his eyes, wrong became permissible.

Saul, the first king of Israel, made the same mistake. God had just given him victory over an extremely wicked land. The Almighty's instructions were simple: "Destroy everything." It was clear He didn't want any trace of evil left.

But Saul began to rationalize. *Surely God wouldn't want us to waste the fattest sheep. I think it would be okay to keep the best cattle . . . for God . . . and maybe a little for me.* It seemed to make sense. He would give some of these prize animals as an offering to the Lord.

When we act in disobedience to God, however, we're playing with fire. Saul's sin wasn't illogical. It wasn't that he couldn't make sense out of what he did—his sin was that he disobeyed God!

Even Christians often rationalize, "This makes sense, so I'll do it!"

Who cares if it makes sense or not? The issue is, are we obeying God?

God doesn't always make sense: *The first shall be last. The last shall be first. Lose your life to find it. Give away to receive.*

It's not our responsibility to understand God. Our responsibility is to simply **OBEY.** And when we, like Josh and Saul, try to make the wrong make sense, we're on dangerous ground.

So don't cheat, okay? God has **BIGGER** plans for you!

Not ALL teachers love teaching.

Gayle just sort of **fell** into teaching because she was pressured to decide an area of concentration in college. One of her professors encouraged her to think about teaching.

"Whomever you marry and wherever you live," he said, "there will always be a demand for teachers." **Sounded good.** After all, everybody has to go to school, right? And for Gayle, teaching meant a steady job. Always. So she pursued a degree in math and secondary education (which meant she could teach on the junior high or high school level).

She landed a teaching job after college graduation and began teaching eighth-grade math. But since she didn't have any experience with teenagers, she was often frustrated.

"They think the whole world revolves around them," she says today. "And they're so rude! Sometimes I'm so angry, I think I'm going to explode."

Gayle has been teaching for fifteen years now. And though she doesn't really **enjoy** her career, it's a job. "I feel as if I'm trapped," she says. "I have two children, and my husband doesn't make enough money in *his* job to support the whole family, so I feel as though I *have* to teach. It's too late to begin again and try to find something I'd really *enjoy* doing."

You might have a teacher like Gayle. And if so, it's obvious—isn't it—that the one running your classroom would much rather run away. Maybe it doesn't seem fair that *you* got stuck with a teacher like *that*. But instead of making matters worse, why not focus on some things **YOU** can do to make the situation better?

1. Care to compliment. You may be the only student in school doing this, but if she looks nice, **TELL HER.** No, you don't have to be gushy about it, but if she's wearing a new dress, and it looks nice, say something. Or if class was enjoyable today, thank her on your way out the door.

2. Stand apart. When the other students are rallying together about what a bad teacher he is, refuse to join the gossip. Yes, you may stand alone, but why be a part of something that won't accomplish anything good?

3. Obey her class rules. If she doesn't allow gum-chewing in class, don't try to get around it. Assigned seating? Then why sneak and sit in another's seat? You can make her job **a LOT** easier if you simply comply with what she says. And, no, that doesn't mean you have to **AGREE** with her rules—just follow them.

4. Surprise him! Want to make a positive difference in his life, and make his job a little easier at the same time? Consider ordering him a one-year gift subscription to *Teacher in Focus*—a monthly magazine for teachers published by Focus on the Family.

Some teachers LOVE teaching.

Take Jennifer Bergland, for instance. We were college roommates, and immediately following graduation, she landed a teaching job. Even though she once had dreams of being a lawyer, she loves teaching so much, she doesn't want to take time off to attend law school.

Not only were Jennifer's parents teachers, but all three of their children became teachers as well. Jennifer's husband *also* teaches! Yep, it's in their blood. For *her*, **teaching isn't simply a job; it's what pushes the blood through her veins.** "I love everything about teaching," she says. "I love getting to know new teens every year. I love the creative challenge of making a required subject interesting. I enjoy this whole process of learning and passing it on to those around me. I love making a difference in kids' lives. I love getting inside the minds of my students—causing them to act and react. There's nothing else in the world I'd rather be doing."

Some of you probably have teachers just like Jennifer. They're in your class every day because they *want* to be. **Don't take them for granted.** They are the kind of people most students try to find ten years after graduation . . . just to say "thanks." Don't wait. Tell her *today*. You may never have another teacher like her again.

Learn to see your teachers as real PEOPLE.

After all, they have feelings, too. Sometimes they get up on the wrong side of the bed, have a low-grade fever (yet come to school anyway), are overloaded with bills to pay, and wonder about their effectiveness.

Some of my favorite memories of teaching school are of students speaking to me in the hallway between classes or just stopping by to hang out in my room before and after school. You see, these are the times when students don't have to speak to their teachers, and aren't even **expected** to. Yet when you do, you're showing your teacher that you enjoy her as a real person. Go ahead. Try it. **We triple-dog-dare you.** Say "hi" to one of your teachers in the hallway. Stop by another teacher's class before or after school and try to carry on a conversation that has nothing to do with school. You might be surprised at what you learn!

6. It's okay to feel WEIRD about taking a shower in P.E. class.

(Okay, we admit the next couple of pages mostly concern **GIRLS.** We even wrote them from a girl's point of view. Guys, it's okay if *you* feel weird, too. If you wanna read this, go ahead—just pretend it's from a guy's perspective. If taking showers in gym class is no big deal to you, flip over to the next chapter.)

Help! I'm in P.E. and I Have to Take a Shower.

If it feels **WEIRD,** you're normal!

11 A.M. MONDAY (AT SCHOOL)

You're standing on the sidelines at Western Oaks School watching your classmates speed up and down the court. They're shooting baskets, dribbling, passing, working on all the skills you've been learning in P.E. class. Everyone's having fun except *you*. It's the fifth time this grading period that you've forgotten your gym clothes. Well . . . you didn't actually *forget* them. **You kinda sorta left your P.E. stash at home.**

But you *love* shooting hoops. And deep inside you wish *you* were on the court laughing and sweating with your friends. And two days ago your mom received Mrs. Bohn's warning notice informing her that you're in danger of failing P.E. So what's going on here?

3:25 P.M. (AT HOME)

"Gym? Gyyymm?!!" Mom pronounces the word as though it's two and holds on to the *m* as if it's stuck to her lips. She's waving the flimsy yellow slip of paper between her fingers as you walk into the kitchen.

"How could you be failing *gym?*" she says with the same astonished, quizzical look she uses when you don't dust and vacuum your room. "I didn't see yesterday's mail until this morning or we would've had this talk sooner. **How in the world can you be failing gym?"**

She raises her voice along with her eyebrows. After you make a few excuses about how hard Coach Barrow pushes you, and how *different* gym class is from the P.E. you had a few years ago in grade school, she puts the warning notice down, looks you square in the eyes, and asks you to come clean.

"Fess up. You never fail *anything*. And you *love* sports. What's going on?"
Good grief! How can you explain this?

8:40 P.M. MONDAY [IN YOUR ROOM]

The stiff, brand-new Spanish text lies open on your bed. The verbs aren't getting conjugated, though, and the questions aren't getting answered. White spaces and skinny blue lines stare back at you from your spiral notebook, and you can't help wishing you'd told Mom how much you hate the whole locker-room scene. **No privacy. No space. Everyone staring at you.** Life used to be so much easier.

But you know what she'd say. "Oh, honey. You're so pretty! You have absolutely nothing to worry about."

Good grief! Why can't she just read my mind, you think. *Doesn't she know how embarrassed I am about my legs and hips?* **Everyone else is a toothpick, and I just know they're all staring at my thighs** . . . *not to mention my tiny bra! And, well . . . it just feels* **weird** *to be naked in front of others.*

Last week the towel slipped, and you were **MAJORLY** embarrassed. You hate taking showers, but if you don't, everyone can smell you a mile away. Why does it have to be so hard?

● ● ● ● ●

This is definitely a dilemma. But the stats are in, and the results prove true: Ninety-nine percent of your locker-room comrades feel exactly as *you* do. It's tough to undress in front of people—and even tougher to stay undressed in front of them long enough to take a shower. **Yikes! And the one percent who act as if they don't mind probably really do mind;** they're just *pretending* they don't!

So, let's figure this out together, okay? I say we come up with a strategy. You go grab a bag of chips (or carrots if you're on a health-kick), and I'll suggest some practical tips.

1. Settle on a system. Organization does wonders!

Have a separate tote bag for gym clothes, and use a smaller carryall for your personal hygiene stuff. Easy access to soap, deodorant, powder, and clean underclothes will make a world of difference. If you're not fumbling around for your underwear, it'll be *on* and you'll be dressed before you know it!

2. Bag a beach towel. Who says you have to use those pint-sized white towels?

Find a bright, funky beach towel you're proud of. A wraparound terry is incredible. Tuck it in (toga-style) and slip on your undies underneath. Prehook your bra, then slip it on over your head as you would a dress. (I promise you can do this. I've tried it!) You're feeling cool and smelling great. *Yes!*

3. Study the shower scene. The fact that everyone else is soaping up isn't a good enough reason to make yourself uncomfortable. Rethink it.

If you showered before you left for school, and if you didn't exert yourself very much, consider just freshening up a bit.

Reapply your deodorant and use a fragrant body powder under your arms. Wash your face, reapply your makeup, and spray a dash of your favorite cologne on your palms.

4. Sizzle with self-confidence. This is **DEFINITELY** the key to feeling better about gym class, undressing, and showering. I know, I know, I know. You're thinking, *Great. How in the world can I learn to feel better about myself? I mean, I have to* **LOOK** *good to* **FEEL** *good!*

No, you don't. Psalm 139:14 says you are fearfully and *wonderfully* made. **When God created your body, He created a good thing.** A *good* thing!

You are a unique and incredible individual, created by the Author of life. If someone looks at you weird when you're changing in the locker room, guess what? It's *her* problem, not yours. Realize that *she's* insecure about who she is and doesn't know the One who can fill her with confidence and security. So pray for her. Here's the bottom line: God doesn't love thin people more than thick ones, or blondes more than brunettes.

A perfect body (whatever perfect means at the moment) **isn't what pleases God. He's looking for a perfect heart.** When He looks at you, He thinks you're beautiful. Really.

This article by Stephanie Bennett first appeared in the September 1994 issue of Brio *magazine.*

7. Learn to submit to AUTHORITY.

Believe it or not, this will actually help you be more successful in life. There's not an employer in the world who will keep someone who always thinks he's right, is constantly trying to "beat the system," or struggles with submitting to those in charge.

Danny was one of the smartest students I've (Susie) ever had in class. He made friends easily, was a natural leader, and had a lot of good ideas. Sound like potential for being the teacher's pet? Hardly. Most of the teachers in our school actually *dreaded* having him in class. Why? Because Danny always thought he was right. **And nobody enjoys being around a know-it-all.**

Often, when he missed an essay question on a test, he'd argue the point; it was as if he were trying to win a case or something. Most teachers are overworked and underpaid and quickly lose respect for students who want to "fight" constantly about every disagreement. Now, please understand—I'm *not* suggesting you keep silent if one of your answers is really correct and has accidentally been counted wrong. You deserve the credit, and your teacher needs to know. And, yes, every teacher makes mistakes. **But simply arguing for the sake of argument, or because you have this innate need to always win, only frustrates those around you.**

Danny went on to college and again appeared to really have his act together on the outside—class president, student-body president, scholarships, fun dates—but on the inside he was still determined to be in control of everything around him.

He graduated with honors and landed a great job. After a year, though, he was looking for other employment. Why? **Because NO ONE enjoys being around someone who can't be submissive to those in authority.** He was always questioning his bosses about procedure. Danny thought his ideas were better than those the company had successfully incorporated for ten years.

Again, please understand, I'm not suggesting that you squelch a great idea or refuse to act on your impulses once in a while. But there's a difference between sharing a new concept or asking permission to try doing things differently, and simply forging ahead, declaring your ways are more effective, more efficient, and more innovative than your supervisor's.

The sooner you can learn to respect—**really respect**—those in authority, the better you'll get along with people, and the more successful you'll be.

8. Don't ask UNNECESSARY questions.

Constantly asking the same questions over and over, like, "Will this be on the test? What page did you say? Is this something we need to remember? How do you spell that?" can be very annoying to a teacher.

Every instructor likes to believe that what he is teaching is important. When you ask questions like this, it makes him feel as though you're only interested in listening if you *have* to. (And for some of you who are reading this, that may be true.) But when a teacher hears you ask unnecessary questions like these, he may begin to see you as "flaky"—someone who's merely there for the ride.

And you don't really want that, do you? Nah. **You want your teachers to see you as dependable, trustworthy, someone they enjoy having in class.** So don't ask unnecessary questions, and when you do ask questions, think before you open your mouth.

Don't be afraid to use school counselors.

After all, they're getting paid really **AVERAGE** dollars to be there for **YOU.** Believe it or not, most would like to do more than just rearrange your class schedule when you don't like a certain teacher. They're also trained to listen, give advice, help you with college information and scholarships, show you how to get the most out of your high-school education, and can even offer advice on major personal problems as well.

Everyone's fear, of course, is that if he's seen talking to a counselor, he must have a problem. Well, sometimes that's true. My school counselor called me (Greg) into his office one day because my grades were slipping. I expected a lecture, but what I got was a friendly guy who was genuinely concerned about my future. He knew more than I did how important a high-school diploma was. He asked me a few really good questions. Unfortunately, I played dumb and pretended nothing was wrong. The truth was, my mother had remarried, moved away to another city, and I was living with my dad—and his girlfriend. It was a very weird time. **I needed help, but thought I was "above" that sort of stuff.**

If you're struggling with something specific, go ahead and make an appointment with a school counselor. It can't ever hurt—and it just might help!

Eat breakfast EVERY morning.

We're serious, mon! Any doctor in the world will tell you **this is THE most important meal of the day.** When you skip it, you start to get hungry around nine A.M., and it's **really, really** hard to concentrate on conjugating verbs when your stomach is talking to everyone in the class.

It's okay if you're not a **BIG** breakfast eater. **Try something simple:** Pop Tarts, a boiled egg, a bowl of cereal, a cup of hot chocolate, oatmeal, a biscuit or bagel, or even a glass of orange juice and a slice of toast with your favorite jelly on top. You'll be surprised not only at how much more **AWAKE** you seem but also at how much more alert you are in your morning classes.

And you know what? I'll bet the people around you will notice the difference, too!

Don't DRAIN your brain.

Sign up for at least one fun class each semester—

something that will give you a fun boost during the day. Wish you knew more about cars? How about a class in auto mechanics? Or maybe you'd enjoy golfing, swimming, creative writing, yearbook, or aerobics.

But don't do what I (Greg) **did** in high school. My senior year I signed up for two different P.E. classes and P.E. help. Instead of learning something that would actually benefit me later in life—woodshop, auto shop, metal shop—I wasted those hours so I could do something easy. Bad move.

My senior year of high school, I (Susie) took a one-semester class called Careers. I loved it! It was **a no-brainer** class that was extremely interesting. We learned about all kinds of various careers, took fun quizzes that helped us see which vocations interested us and which jobs we'd more than likely be successful in, and watched a variety of fun films and heard great speakers all promoting different careers. It was a class I definitely enjoyed, yet it was also a class that helped me think about careers I'd never thought about before.

We learned how to research different options and found out how much we could start earning in various vocations. It was fascinating!

Go ahead! You deserve a break. Sign up for some fun classes that will **spark your imagination,** and classes you'll enjoy attending.

Make the MOST of your study halls and library times so you can have fun when you go home.

Sure, sometimes during the day your brain needs a breather. But think about it: **What's the last thing you want to do** when you get home? (Okay, besides vacuum and dust the garage.) **HOMEWORK,** right? Some teachers will always require homework, but many only assign about thirty minutes a day. If you finish it at school during your breaks and planned study times, then you don't even have to think about it when you get home.

Our advice: Take the hours of the day when your brain is actually functioning—school hours—to get as much done as you can.

BE ON TIME TO CLASS

14. Refuse to GOSSIP.

Yeah, it's tough. For help on ending this habit, read on.

TEN CURES FOR THE CHRONIC GOSSIP:

A practical peek at what it takes to snap your trap.

Gossip is powerful stuff. Whether you're *starting* or merely *spreading* gossip, you're controlling what someone thinks about another. When you *listen* to gossip, you suddenly receive a strange form of prestige: You're enrolled in an exclusive class of people called "those who know."

Yet the price for this kind of power and prestige is high. Gossip cheapens a friendship and makes it hard to establish close relationships. And if that's not enough, **God isn't too hot on gossip,** either. In fact, He has a special word for it . . . **sin!**

But you *know* all these things. What you *don't* know is how to stop. If gossip is a habit you can't seem to break, try these tested-and-proven gossip busters:

1. Change the subject. Reporters and talk-show hosts are masters at turning the course of a conversation without a fuss. Watch a talk-show host steer a guest from one topic to another: "You know, before I forget, I want to ask you this. . . ." The guest is now on to a new topic, and the old subject is left quietly in the dust. When you catch yourself in a circle of gossip, grab the wheel and steer the conversation to a new topic.

2. Walk away. When you can't control the course of a conversation that turns to gossip, just make an excuse and leave. This amazing little trick will save you (many times in your life) from greater harms than gossip. *Now* is a great time to begin practicing it.

3. Say stop. You have the right to choose what you hear. Unfortunately, ears don't come equipped with flaps. (Some *hats* come with earflaps, but unless you live in the Arctic Circle, these usually clash with your outfit.) To stop up your hearing, you have to cut off the noise at the source. It's okay to say, "Please don't tell me." Eventually, people will figure out that you're not into gossip, and they won't try to involve you.

4. Card yourself. The apostle Paul knew the powerful connection between our thoughts and our actions. To help us direct our thoughts, he gave us this very cool advice: *Whatever is true, whatever is noble, whatever is right, whatever is pure, whatever is lovely, whatever is admirable—if anything is excellent or praiseworthy—think about such things* (Philippians 4:8, NIV).

Here's how this verse can help you **break your gossip habit.** Pick out all the positive words from the verse and write them on an index card (TRUE, NOBLE, RIGHT, PURE, LOVELY, ADMIRABLE, EXCELLENT, PRAISEWORTHY). Carry the card in your pocket or purse.

As you pick up the phone or walk up to greet someone, quickly review the list. Before you open your mouth, check to be sure the words in your brain are compatible with the words from the list. It's tough to gossip and praise at the same time!

5. Announce your mistake. If you catch yourself in the middle of a sentence that's going to come out as gossip, stop yourself and say, "You know, I was about to gossip, and I've decided to stop, so I'm done talking." Your friends are going to look at you funny (and you're going to look at *yourself* funny), but the important issue is that you're going to avoid this awkward situation as often as possible.

6. Make a pact. It's always easier to change a habit when you have a friend to do it with. Talk about your habit, what it will take to break it, and how you can encourage each other to stop.

7. Pay a fine. If you have friends who are willing to quit the gossip habit with you, agree on a system of consequences: If you're caught gossiping, the one who catches you gets a quarter. If you're a major-league gossip, raise the fine to a dollar.

8. Find "inside" friends. Inside friends are the ones who care about what goes on inside a person and give little attention to appearances. If your circle of friends has become a gossip fest, seek out people who don't make gossip the focus of friendship. After all, gossip is a team game—and if your team refuses to play, you won't be playing the game either.

9. Fess up. If you can't seem to break a gossip habit, make a deal with your close friends. If they catch you gossiping, you must go to the person who was the subject of your gossip and apologize for talking behind his or her back! Two or three humiliating apologies will probably cure you.

10. Get drastic. If, after trying all the above, you *still* catch yourself gossiping, immediately throw your purse, schoolbooks, lunch, or whatever else you're holding into the air. Then proceed through a repertoire of sounds from barnyard animals. Once should be enough to cure you.

As you're struggling to overcome the gossip habit, you can **rejoice that the One who knows you better than anyone**—who knows every sin and dark secret you've ever held inside—**has never gossiped about you . . .** and never will. That's right. God knows it all, and if He wanted to, He could blab your sins and secrets all over town.

But instead of announcing them, He chooses to *forget* them! Or, as He puts it, "I, even I, am he who blots out your transgressions, for my own sake, and remembers your sins no more" (Isaiah 43:25, NIV).

If God can know *everything* and still choose to forget our sins, **maybe we can learn to forget the shortcomings of others.** And the rumor is we *can* do it!

This article by Todd Temple first appeared in the July 1994 issue Brio *magazine.*

Do your HOMEWORK.

Why? Because . . .
a. it's the right thing to do.
b. you really WILL need to know the area where American author William Faulkner grew up (Yoknapatawpha County) later in life. (Hey, it could happen! Okay, let's say you're a contestant on some game show about ten years from now. Who knows? That could very well be the $10 million bonus question. And you'd miss out just because you didn't do your eleventh-grade English homework. We couldn't let you hold that against us. So **just do it!**)

c. if you don't do it, you'll be tempted to cheat. And consistent cheaters are often-times tempted to steal cheap jewelry from department stores. And probably by the seventh time you attempt to steal something, you'll get caught. And when your pastor finds out you've been arrested, how do you think he's going to feel knowing he let you work in the nursery one Sunday? He'll feel pretty low. So lousy, that he'll probably resign the pastorate and move far away. And when your church falls apart, who do you think the congregation is going to blame? **YOU!** And with that much blame and guilt being heaped upon you, **it's only a matter of time before you crack like an egg.** And when a person cracks, what happens? They're usually hauled downtown for intensive psychological therapy. Which means you're going to be spending **LOTS** of time with people in small rooms who think they're Napoleon, or insist that the carpet under their feet can actually carry them to worlds yet unconquered. And **when you finally are released,** do you really think you're going to be able to land a job as anything more than just a cereal-taster? We think not. So, there you have it. Don't do your homework, and eat cereal the rest of your life!

d. it provides discipline . . . and even though that's a yuk word, **it really DOES help** you become more consistent in other areas of your life.

e. if you don't, someone will always find out (your teacher, your parents, the President of the United States . . . Okay, maybe not, but stick with us—we're trying to make a point here).

f. it's God's will. (Can't argue with that, now, can you? See, that's the fun part of writing a book. The authors always get **the last word.**)

16 ⦃ Not all kids have a solid FOUNDATION for their lives, therefore, many make bad choices.

Don't get sucked into that. Establish your self-esteem and your happiness in a foundation that will **NOT** move . . . Jesus Christ. If you establish and maintain a strong relationship with the Lord, others can't help but notice the difference. And guess what? They'll want what you have!

Not only that, but when your world crashes around you, you will still have a solid foundation in God. So if your parents separate or even divorce, if your friends say unkind things about you behind your back, or if that special guy or girl just won't give you the time of day . . . your hope and your reason for living remains steady. NOTHING can shake a strong foundation on Christ, the solid rock.

Need a reminder? How 'bout taping the words to this wonderful hymn in your locker? Or cut it out and use it as a bookmark? Or better yet, try memorizing it! You'll be surprised at how much **strength** you'll gain from the meaning of the words when you reflect on it throughout a hectic day.

The Solid Rock

My hope is built on nothing less than Jesus' blood and righteousness.

I dare not trust the sweetest frame, but wholly lean on Jesus' name.

On Christ, the solid Rock, I stand;

all other ground is sinking sand. All other ground is sinking sand.

When darkness seems to hide His face, I rest on His unchanging grace.

In every high and stormy gale, my anchor holds within the veil.

On Christ, the solid Rock, I stand; **all other ground is sinking sand.**

All other ground is sinking sand.

His oath, His covenant, His blood, support me in the whelming flood.

When all around my soul gives way,

He then is all my Hope and Stay.

On Christ, the solid Rock, I stand; all other ground is sinking sand.

All other ground is sinking sand.

When He shall come with trumpet sound, oh may I then in Him be found.

Dressed in His righteousness alone, faultless to stand before the throne.

On Christ, the solid Rock, I stand; all other ground is sinking sand.

All other ground is sinking sand.

Words by Edward Mote, 1834; music by William B. Bradbury, 1863.

Try not to get so caught up in a PART-TIME JOB that it affects your schoolwork and activities.

You'll have the rest of your life to work! When I (Susie)

was a youth minister, Brent was one of the most involved kids in my youth group.
He was definitely a leader, and everyone respected him.

But when he got his license at age sixteen, he suddenly decided he wanted a
car. His parents told him that if he'd get a part-time job and pay for the insurance
and half the car payments, they'd match the rest and help him buy a vehicle.

Well, that's all the motivation he needed! He diligently searched the want
ads and finally landed a job. He worked almost every day after school as well as
Saturdays and almost every Sunday. **You can guess what that did to his church
involvement, can't you?** He stopped attending our weekly discipleship group. (He
had to work.) And he quit coming to our **big-bang** midweek youth
evangelistic outreach. (He was on the job.) And he only made it to Sunday ser-
vices about twice a month.

I often wondered why his parents dangled such an attractive carrot in front
of his face. (I mean, **what kid wouldn't want a car** if his parents offered to help him
buy it and make half the car payments?) From my viewpoint, however, Brent was
sacrificing much more than simple church attendance. His
spiritual growth suffered. His **friendships** with good
Christian kids from the youth group declined, and he was always tired.

I tried to help him realize that he'd have the rest of his life to work, earn
money, and purchase a car. When he could have borrowed his parents' car any
time he wanted, was it really that essential that he have his own vehicle?

Once you get off track from being deeply involved in church and church activities, **it's hard to get back on.** I'm convinced that Brent would be a strong churchman today (would probably be helping with the youth, teaching a Sunday school class, or serving as a church board member or deacon) if he hadn't been so anxious to give it all up for some wheels.

Enjoy your teen years while you can! If you've got to work, **go easy!** You'll have the rest of your life to work and earn a living.

Get involved in at least one
EXTRACURRICULAR activity.

Why? Because you'll learn important social skills, make more friends, develop wider interests and abilities, look good on your college entrance applications, and become a well-rounded person who has a broad spectrum of interests. **Best of all, it's FUN!**

19 Use your LOCKER.

You really don't have to lug a ton of stuff to every class. That's what lockers are for. So use 'em. Make your locker your "home away from home." Decorate it, let it reflect you. **Make a statement to others with it.**

Brianna hangs 3 x 5 note cards with **Scripture** on them inside her locker. "It helps keep me focused on what's really important every time I open it," she says.

Grayson has a few photos of **sports celebs** inside his locker door. "When I'm feeling tense or having a bad day, it helps to open my locker and look at some of the people I admire," he says.

Open Jon's locker, and you'll find **cartoons and comics** plastered inside. "They make me smile," he says. "I'll be bummed because I didn't do well on a test, or maybe someone snubbed me in the hallway, and I'll open my locker and can't help but laugh."

What can you put in *your* locker? Well, that depends. Even though it *is* your personal, private zone, it *doesn't* mean you can store harmful stuff inside. Weapons, drugs, and anything questionable doesn't belong in your locker. Use this specific space to **create a BRIGHT spot** in your day.

Have a few notes from friends that always lift you up? Your locker's a great place to keep them. What about your Bible? When your teacher gives you some free time at the end of the day, you can zero in on words of encouragement from your Creator—if you have your Bible at school.

Think about your interests and **what makes you smile . . .** and bring some of those fun things from home to stash in your locker. You'll be surprised at how much better your day at school can be when you have a little bit of home inside your locker.

Button your buttons and zip your zipper

(It's smart to check these things at least once a day!)

21. Be a good LISTENER.

Everyone loves being around someone who's a good listener. It's a special way of making others feel important. **Want a lot of friends?** Learn to listen!

When you listen . . . **really listen . . .** you may hear some bitterness between sarcastic remarks from Joey, the school clown. You might find out that Amber's dad left the family last week. Jeremy's mom has cancer. Nicole's father lost his job. Brandon's brother just got arrested . . . again.

And when you hear about things that are hard to handle, **you have an opportunity to encourage** some hurting friends. And that's exactly what Jesus calls us to do, isn't it? To **be a bright light** in a dark world. To offer hope and love to those who can't see beyond tomorrow.

And **you can** do that . . . if you'll strive to become a good listener. Want to know how to develop good listening skills?

1. Ask good questions. This involves conversation that requires more than simply *yes* or *no* answers. Instead of saying, "Hey, Amy, didja have a good weekend?" say, "Hey, Amy! What were the best and worst parts of your weekend?" You'll learn a whole lot more!

2. Learn to read between the lines.

If Ashley is normally an easy-going friend, but is suddenly acting distant and giving you short, cold comebacks, don't focus on what she's *saying*. **Zero in, instead, on what she's not saying.** "Ashley, how are things at home? Do you need some help studying for that history test tomorrow? How's your brother?" By digging for information, you'll probably stumble on what's *really* bothering your friend and can offer to listen and help.

3. Don't be afraid of silence. There's a girl in my Sunday school class who's really a fun person and often wants to grab a burger or a Coke with me. And even though I usually go, I **always** dread it. Know why? Because she never stops talking! I'm completely worn out after being around her only a few minutes. She's totally uncomfortable with silence. Sometimes I just want to scream, "Chill out, will ya? We don't *always* have to have a conversation going!"

Learn to appreciate the silence, because it's during the pauses of your conversations that friends have a chance to reflect, think, ask deeper questions, or simply enjoy your company.

Avoid the COMPARISON game.

Heather wears the latest fashions, and you've never owned a name-brand piece of clothing in your life. Eric is the star quarterback, and you've only *dreamed* of making the team. David makes straight *A's* without even cracking a book. You study for three hours straight and end up with a *C*. What's the deal? **Comparing yourself to those around you will NEVER bring fulfillment.** It **WILL** cause jealousy, bitterness, and anger to take root inside your head and heart. Strive to quietly trust yourself to your Creator, and He'll help you develop your unique abilities. That's what contemporary Christian artist Lisa Bevill did. Here's her story.

Lisa Bevill: A Christie Brinkley Wannabe? NOT! (anymore)

Recognize these lyrics? "Double-double your refreshment. Double-double your enjoyment. No single gum double-freshens your mouth like double-fresh Doublemint gum."

Hard to believe that the girl singing these words was **double-double unhappy** during her teen years. Behind the sugary-sweet voice that has since made the commercial a familiar hum-along lived a girl filled with self-doubt, depression, and even thoughts of suicide.

Lisa Bevill struggled with something *you* may be facing, too: **trying to live up to the "perfect body."**

THE COMPARISON KILLER

"I'd pick up *Seventeen* magazine," Lisa remembers, "and just stare at super-model Christie Brinkley. I'd practically gag because I wanted so badly to look like her."

Thumbing through the pages month after month, Lisa became acutely aware of every blemish and imperfection she carried. With tears streaming down her face, she couldn't help but wonder why *she* couldn't look like Christie.

"I'd glare at her body in envy. But **no matter how hard I exercised or dieted, I just couldn't do it,**" Lisa says. "So I felt like a failure. I hated my thighs, my stomach, everything about me. Christie was beautiful and popular, and I wanted what she had. **More than anything else in life, I wanted to be liked and accepted.**"

Lisa stored her anger and warped feelings deep inside, but the frustration grew. As she stood in front of her bedroom mirror, her heart often screamed, "You're ugly! How can you be so fat?"

On the **outside** Lisa was every parent's dream: excited about church, doing well in school, playing the piano for her youth choir. But on the **inside,** she was slowly falling apart. No one knew that behind the perky smile lived a frightened, depressed teenage girl.

"Nobody knew I needed help," she admits. "Everyone thought, **'She's got it all together,'** because I made sure I painted that picture."

BAD TIMES GET WORSE

Though Lisa came from a terrific family, it was filled with heart-ripping troubles: Both her parents were seriously ill. Imagine her heartbreak at age twelve when she learned that her mom had cancer.

"It was devastating," Lisa recalls. **"We lived on an emotional roller coaster.** We didn't know whether she'd live six months, two years . . . or two weeks.

"I was scared!" Lisa says. "No one wants to be orphaned. **Though I knew my parents loved me, I couldn't help but worry** about the day when I'd be all alone. I just wanted to feel secure . . . like we'd all be together forever, but I was scared to death."

As she cried her prayers to God, she often wondered if this would be the last prayer she would pray for her mom or dad.

Her dad lived with the agonizing pain of rheumatoid arthritis. He died when she was just nineteen years old. **"It was a sudden thing,"** she says. "The arthritis had crippled his hands and feet to the point where they were bent and twisted. One afternoon he called to Mom—who was in the next room—and said, —'I think I'm going to faint.'

"When I heard him calling, I immediately rushed to his room. He had collapsed on the floor, so I bent over and cradled him in my arms. Seconds later, he was dead."

Lisa's mom died just a few years later—the day after Lisa returned from her honeymoon. "It was so hard," she recalls. **"I didn't know how to deal with all the emotions** I'd collected over the years."

Rainbows Through the Storm

"The comparison thing mixed with the unknown of my parents' health was slowly killing me on the inside," Lisa admits. "It was hindering me from seeing all the **positive** things about myself: a girl with a ton of potential. When **I began to see myself through God's eyes** instead of my own, the depression started to lift."

Lisa began learning that **God loved her exactly the way she was.** A counselor helped her wade through the baggage, all the feelings she'd kept inside . . . stuff like not measuring up, the fear of being abandoned, depression, even thoughts of suicide.

"I got to a point of telling myself, 'You'll *never* look like Christie Brinkley. You're five feet six—forget about being six feet tall.'

"I actually looked at every part of my body and said, 'You know what? I love you, and I'm gonna try to make you better than you are. But I'm not going to knock myself out trying to look like this month's cover girl.'"

As Lisa allowed God to heal her damaged self-concept, other benefits occurred as well. **Her spiritual life began to blossom,** her faith deepened, and she became more confident in the talents God had blessed her with.

The Big Payoff

Today Lisa's a happily married wife and the mother of two children. She still has tough days, but now there's a difference. She likes herself. She's content. **She's fulfilling God's dreams for her life.**

Lisa has two albums under her wings: *My Freedom* and *All Because of You.*

Her involvement in contemporary Christian music sort of happened through the "back door."

Church music played a big role in her life during high school, and after graduation she began auditioning for jingles in Nashville.

If you often catch yourself humming along with familiar TV commercials, then chances are you have even sung *with* her! **Recognize this?** "I love what you do for me, Toyota!" And you can smack along with this one: "You get extra flavor, extra fun with Extra sugar-free gum!"

Lisa's also done a Domino's pizza jingle, a diet Orange Crush tune, and several more you'd recognize. Producer Brown Bannister (who's also worked with Amy Grant and several other Christian artists) got wind of this energetic talent and signed her as his premier artist on a brand-new label: Vireo Records (a division of Sparrow).

LESSONS FROM THE PAST

Now that her future looks bright, how does it feel to flash back to those painfully shy school days? "I've learned that even though time can't erase the hurtful memories, I don't carry around a bunch of bitterness. **Harboring all that sadness would only cripple me,**" says Lisa.

"Occasionally I bump into a few of my high school classmates who still live in the Nashville area," she continues. "The football players and the guys in the big cliques who wouldn't give me the time of day **then** are suddenly paying all kinds of attention to me **now.** I just want to scream, 'You snobs. You're so shallow!' Of course, I don't," Lisa says, laughing.

"But I sometimes feel like saying, 'Okay, so I learned how to do my hair; I learned how to wear makeup—big deal. **Dare to look past the surface.**'"

Lisa's also learned that performance isn't the key to acceptance. "I always felt if I performed just right, everyone would like me. I *now* know that **the only person I need to be performing (or living) for is the Lord.** Whew! That sure takes a lot of pressure off," she says. "It feels so good to finally realize that God accepts me *just as I am!*"

This article by Susie Shellenberger first appeared in the 1993 September issue of Brio *magazine.*

23} Don't get BRANDED as one of those students who is always asking to go to the bathroom or get a drink of water.

Many times, a teacher interprets this as manipulation—as simply trying to get out of class. (And yes, **a teacher can usually tell** when you're serious and **when you really HAVE to go.)**

SURPRISE everyone by doing what's right.

This includes:

- **Respecting the opposite sex.**

- Not dressing provocatively.

- Refusing to spread gossip.

- Being **POSITIVE.**

- Not telling off-color jokes.

- **Being friendly to people** everyone else makes fun of.

- Handing out genuine compliments.

- Being honest. (Not even telling **little white lies.**)

- Being polite to those around you. (Don't interrupt. Laugh *with* your friends but not *at* them. **Believe and expect the best from those around you.**)

If you're REEEEALLY sick, stay home.

No one at school wants what you have!

But if all you have is a sore throat or cramps, **don't be a wimp.**

Be willing to say "I'M SORRY."

When you're wrong, learn to admit it. **Teachers AND friends will respect you a LOT if you'll simply admit it when you've blown it** instead of trying to make excuses or cover it up.

My junior year I (Greg) had to take an English lit. class. It was awful! We had to actually read a book! Well, I hated reading and so far had escaped high school without reading even one whole book. I chose to read *The Autobiography of Malcolm X.* I got about halfway through (it was actually pretty interesting), then quit. When it came time to do the book report, **I faked my way through it.** When my teacher called me in after school, I didn't know why.

"Greg, I have your book report here on my desk," he said. "I have to tell you that I don't believe you finished the book. Is there anything I need to know?"

"I finished the book, Mr. Smith, **honest."** I was lying of course. (Hey, I wasn't a Christian, I didn't know any better!) He smiled and disagreed. I emphatically stuck to my guns that I had finished. He was cool about it and didn't actually come out and call me a liar, but I knew **he knew I was lying.** And he knew that I knew that he knew I was lying.

The thing is, if I just would have admitted that I zoned-out on "Star Trek" reruns after school instead of reading, he probably would have given me a second chance. **He didn't want to fail me,** he wanted me to succeed!

Looking back, **the worst part** of the whole episode was . . . he gave me a passing grade in the class. Instead of allowing me to face the music, he slid me by. I needed a wake-up call, but didn't get it.

Write a NOTE to someone who's going through a family tragedy.

Whether you know the person or not, if you hear her grandmother, grandfather, mom, dad, brother, sister . . . whoever, has died or is very ill, **practice some basic Christian skills:** send a card showing your concern and let her know you'll pray for her. It doesn't have to be long or mushy, just **something that communicates the compassion Jesus would have.**

Say THANK YOU to your teachers at the end of the semester or the school year.

You've heard it before, we'll say it again: **teaching is a profession that gets very few thank-you's.** Basically, you're teaching kids who think they know it all, who don't want to be taught, who try to "get by" and not really learn, all for about $26,000 to $36,000 a year.

Most are committed to their students and really do desire to prepare them for life. They don't ask too much of you besides **"do your best."**

A card, a note scratched on old notebook paper, a firm handshake, a genuine smile . . . it doesn't take much. If you **communicate** your appreciation in even a small way, it will make all of their toil **worthwhile.**

If you have a QUESTION about the assignment, ask the teacher—not the kid next to you.

One day when I (Susie) was a junior in high school, my history teacher was really fed up with the class. **"No more talking!"** he demanded. "Now turn to page . . . and start reading!"

Even though I was listening, I didn't hear the page number. I quietly leaned over and asked the girl across the aisle, "What page did he say?"

Mr. Ledbetter *saw* me talking to someone and immediately started yelling at me. "Shellenberger, you can report for detention tomorrow after school!" he said.

After class, I approached him and said, "I know it looked as if I were talking to Peggy, but I really wasn't. **All I did was ask her what page we were supposed to turn to."**

"Well, that's talking, isn't it?" he responded. Even though I continued to plead my case, it didn't do any good. I had been caught. And even though **it didn't seem fair,** the fact was I *had* talked after he specifically said, "No talking." The result? I had to spend an unnecessary half hour after school sitting in a room with angry kids.

It was a hard lesson, but you can bet **the next time** I had a question about the assignment, **I asked the teacher** instead of a friend.

Don't BORROW your friends' clothes.

Yeah, I know. Kendra has a sweater you'd die for. And you really need something special for your date with Geoff Friday night. **Don't risk it.** What happens when you accidentally snag her sweater or spill ketchup on it? Even though she *says* it's okay, chances are you may have damaged the friendship. Permanently. After all, this was really a **special** sweater. Kendra's grandmother gave it to her as a gift when she won the piano contest last year. **Don't take unnecessary chances when it comes to your friendships.** Value friends enough to refrain from borrowing special things from them . . . even when you're tempted to.

Even if it feels uncomfortable, REACH OUT to those around you.

Want more friends? Then **learn to BE friends** with more people around you. What? You say that's uncomfortable? It was for singer Margaret Becker, too. That's right. Waaaay back in junior high, she was really, really shy. But guess what? She *made* herself reach out. Here's her story.

Margaret Becker: School Greeter

Another Monday morning. The same old push and shove to get into the building. Girls chattering about hair spray; boys rehashing Saturday night's football game. You make it inside, and someone standing by the door gives you a big smile and says good morning in a way that's very unusual—especially for a Monday!

Margaret Becker made it to school before everyone else so she could be a greeter, offering a smile and hello to every person who came through the door. **Would you believe she considered herself to be shy?** "Being assertive didn't conquer my shyness," she says. "But it helped me work through it and build friendships. Otherwise, I would've retreated into myself."

Margaret has done just the opposite of retreating; she's become a successful artist in the Christian music scene. But **you could say her lifelong career is in construction.** You see, Margaret spends a lot of time building—confidence, relationships, music skills, and even houses with Habitat for Humanity. Margaret also knows the value of a strong foundation for any building project you undertake—**Jesus Christ.**

Confidence

"There was a turning point for me in junior high," Margaret says. "I realized **either I was going to be intimidated by people** and avoid all uncomfortable situations, **or I was going to be aggressive and make friends.** I'd lean against my locker and talk to people, and I'd even say something to strangers.

"I wasn't very attractive at that point in my life—I had acne and bad hair days just like everyone else. I was kind of a joke around the school, but I almost always got a smile from the people I greeted. I figured they'd make fun of me anyway if I retreated into myself, so **I might as well go ahead and make an effort** to do this."

Margaret got to know *a lot* of people—not just friends from her softball, drama, or music activities. "I'd greet the druggies, the popular crowd, the athletes—everyone who came through the door. Eventually I formed a close group of friends. Being a greeter was **the road to popularity,** if you want to call it that."

Today, Margaret's ability to talk with people is a boost to her work. "I'm still a greeter—so much of my job is meeting people," she says. "And yes, it's still scary at times. But **the more I do it, the more I understand** how to talk to people—what to say and what not to say."

She admits there are some who don't appreciate the friendliness. "There's nothing worse than meeting someone cold and indifferent. But for every person like that, there are ten who're happy you made **the first move** to reach out."

This article by Susan Maffett first appeared in the May 1994 issue of Brio *magazine.*

Be KIND to your teachers—even if you don't like them.

School is a great dress rehearsal for the rest of your life. Think about it. You'll probably have a few coworkers, and even a few employers, whom you really don't like.

Learning to get along now with those who are not easy to be around will really prepare you for handling **tough situations** later in life.

Put a little EXTRA work into your assignments.

When I (Susie) taught high-school speech and drama, I challenged my students to **REFUSE** the easy way. "When you're giving a speech," I said, "do it differently than anyone else. Keep thinking and creating until you have an original presentation."

One of the first assignments I gave was informative speeches. Students would inform us "how to" or "how not to" do something, and actually demonstrate during their presentation.

A few of the more **outstanding** speeches were ones in which students put some extra thought, time, and creativity into their presentation. Chelene received permission to bring her labrador retriever to class, and gave a wonderful speech on "How to Take Care of Your Pet." She hauled in brushes, collar and leash, treats, and enough stuff to open a pet store. It was fun, creative, and very informative. And having a big dog in the classroom was **a memorable experience for ALL of us!**

Mercy dressed in really baggy and sloppy clothes. I had no idea what her speech was going to be about, but my curiosity was already piqued when I saw her enter the classroom and wait to be called. When it was her turn, she grabbed a pail, some rubber gloves, a **TON** of cleaning stuff, and led the entire class down the hall and . . . into the girls' bathroom! (Luckily, she had cleared this with the proper staff ahead of time!) All thirty-four of us crammed inside the bathroom and watched while she demonstrated how to properly clean a bathroom.

It was great! She cleaned the sinks, the toilet, and even started mopping the floor. (The custodial staff loved her!) Again, **it was that extra time and creativity** she had poured into making what *could* have been an ordinary speech **extraordinary** that earned her an *A*.

And Todd came early to school for *his* setup! He rigged some wires and hung a shower curtain over them at the front of the class. It was really fun, because all day long students kept asking me what the shower curtain was for. I had to tell them I didn't know, but I'd find out during fourth-period speech class. That was talked about all day!

Finally, Todd was called on to give his speech, and he set the rest of the area with towels, radio-tape player, a couple of plastic kiddie toys, shampoo, and **soap-on-a-rope.** He then stepped out of the room and pulled off his sweat pants to reveal his swimsuit. He turned the tape player on low (he had recorded running water from his shower at home), and jumped into the "shower." Once inside, he gave a speech that was **hilarious** on "How to Get Ready for School."

About thirty seconds later, he hopped out, wrapped a bathrobe around himself, and began drying and styling his hair. Next, he started foaming up his face and shaved. It was terrific! The whole class howled, he never lost our attention, and of course, he earned an *A* for such a creative presentation.

When *you're* asked to give a speech or an oral presentation, **don't simply settle for what has to be done.** Go the extra mile. You'll be surprised what you can come up with if you really put more time and energy into the assignment. Here are a few other great ideas—just in case *you* have to give an oral presentation for speech class anytime soon:

• Michelle brought in a full-sized thawed-out chicken and showed us how to pull it apart and prepare it for dinner.

• Aaron dressed up like an **exclamation point** and reviewed the proper use of punctuation and grammar.

• Nathan set up his drums.

• Shane drove his car right outside the door and motioned for all of us to gather round while he showed us how to change a tire.

• Jessica brought ingredients for banana cake and showed us how to make it. (An added plus: She also brought in a pre-made banana cake and gave us samples at the conclusion of her speech. **Yummm!)**

• When it was time for a *persuasive* speech, Shellie brought in a beer and drank her way through an entire speech on the dangers of drinking. (She had actually washed an empty beer bottle ahead of time and filled it with Mountain Dew. But since I was the only one who knew this, it was really effective. And yes, she **DID** tell the students what she'd done after the speech was over.)

What could YOU come up with if you really tried? I have a feeling that the *best* speeches are still yet to be created. That means you could even top these! So **go for it.** We believe in you!

34. Be a SURVIVOR.

Stand tall even when you're . . .

- being put down

- laughed at

- made fun of

- **questioned**

- ridiculed

- talked about.

Nine times out of ten, kids make fun of each other because of **the reaction** they get. If you try not to let harsh remarks bother you, chances are the harassing will soon end.

Dare to be JESUS to those around you.

That's what Amy did. And people couldn't help but know there was something wonderfully different about her. You know what? They automatically wanted what she had!

How do you make an impact like that? Well, for starters, Amy wasn't cliquish. Yes, she DID have close friends—people she would rather be with than anyone else—but she was careful not to exclude others. You see, cliques are *natural.* It's only normal for you to want to hang around with those you share common interests with, enjoy being with, and who love *your* company as well. There's nothing wrong with that.

Cliques only become harmful when you exclude others and refuse to let anyone else into your circle. Amy was great at making everyone feel **GOOD** about being around her. **She focused on the needs of the other person** instead of always talking and thinking about herself. And people enjoy being with those who care about them. So naturally everyone wanted to hang out with Amy.

She always seemed happy, too. Not the phony or pretend stuff. Amy experienced some hard times. She definitely had her share of ups and downs. But it was obvious that she liked herself. She felt **GOOD** about who she was. There was **a genuine joyful spirit** about her. And again, people love being around those who are happy. So naturally everyone wanted to hang out with Amy.

But it didn't stop there. When kids said stuff like, "How come you always seem to have it together?" and "What makes you tick?" Amy's face lit up with a smile that wouldn't quit as she responded, "Wanna come to church with me this weekend? I think you'll be surprised. If you'll come with me, I'll fill you in on my secret."

Yep, it worked. And Amy made **an unforgettable impact** on those around her. For some it was an impact that'll last **eternally.**

Every now and then FLEX your fingers.

Believe it or not, **making a fist** a few times each hour will keep your blood circulating freely through your hands.

If you're in a class that does an **exceptional** amount of writing, this will help prevent your fingers from cramping.

Don't be someone who always has an EXCUSE.

Face it. *Sometimes* you just won't have an excuse. **Deal with it.** Students who are constantly trying to make up excuses to explain their unacceptable behavior are usually a teacher's worst nightmare. Here are some excuses that *never* work.

Really, Really, Really Bad Excuses

• What? You mean the A.C.T. and the S.A.T. aren't open-book tests? I'm shocked! I never knew that.

• Well, yeah, I heard you give the homework assignment. I just didn't realize we were supposed to **write out** the answers. I did the work. I really did! **It's just all in my head.**

• Can I go to my locker? Well, you didn't *tell* us to bring our textbook every day!

• I thought semester exams were a group project. Honest, I really did!

• Cheating? No way. **I'd never cheat.** I was just, uh, trying to, um, see the name brand on Sarah's watch. See, I've been working an extra job so I can buy my grandmother one just like it.

• The homework assignment? Well . . . yes . . . I'm aware that I didn't turn it in. You see, Mrs. Foster, **this is really bizarre,** but last night there was, uh, this tornado-thing that swept through our neighborhood, and uh, well, my homework assignment was completely destroyed.

What's that? You live within a mile of my house and didn't hear anything about a tornado? Hmmm. That's interesting, Mrs. Foster. And I believe it just goes to show that Mother Nature acts in unexpected and unexplainable ways.

What's that? You'll expect a five-page typed report with footnotes and research cards on unexplainable acts of Mother Nature to be turned in tomorrow morning? Okay, **can I just be real honest here?** I know this may come as a total shock to you, but I was just kidding. I never actually even **DID** the homework assignment. Is there any possible way I can just turn it in tomorrow even though it'll be a little late?

Tomorrow will be fine? Oh, thanks, Mrs. Foster! You're the best. You really are.

What's that? Along with my five-page typed report on unexplainable acts of Mother Nature, plus a seven-page typed report on the pitfalls of procrastination? Uh, Mrs. Foster, can you give me any information on **military school?**

• But I *wasn't* talking! Okay, yes, I *was* moving my mouth. And yes, sounds *were* emitted from my vocal chords. **But it's not what you think!** You see, I'm trying to learn ventriloquism. It's my only chance for a college scholarship.

• Well, it's not that I'm actually *late*. I'm just really time-sensitive impaired.

• I know it *looks* as though I'm chewing gum, Mr. Fields, but actually I'm simply exercising the bonecular structure of my jaws. **It's a medical thing.**

• Well, no, I wouldn't actually call this a *note* that I'm passing. You see, I'm . . . doing research. Yeah, that's it! I'm gathering information from students who are extremely challenged by your thorough ability of imparting knowledge and am in the process of creating a book proposal on the educational climate of prospective **learning-enhanced** pupils who draw upon that learned behavior of emitting quality results to institutional testing programs.

38 Pay attention!

When Mrs. Hulsey says, "Turn to page 63," don't ask, "In our books?" And all those class announcements? Sometimes they're actually important.

Pay attention!

You'll be surprised at what you might learn.

Some of the kids walking the halls in your school have NEVER been prayed for.

It's hard to imagine what your life would be like if someone—a parent, grandparent, aunts or uncles, neighbors—didn't pray for you. There's no way of knowing where your life would lead, either. Those heartfelt offerings before the Father by those who care about you are the unseen power source of your strength against the forces of darkness.

What would your life be like if NO ONE had ever prayed for you?

Check out the hallways, the smoking section at school, downtown parks where the homeless live. If you're perceptive, you can almost guess which names have rarely, if ever, been brought before God's throne of grace. Their lives show it.

The next time you complain or get disgusted about the looks or behavior of other kids at school, **try to imagine what you could be like** if Satan's forces were never held back from influencing you.

Stick up for the UNDERDOG.

Mark, Steve, and Mike were three guys I (Greg) knew in junior high and high school. They weren't athletes. In fact, two of them were overweight and the other perfectly fit the 98-pound weakling mold. Do you think the other guys left them alone?

Not a chance. After all, **teenage guys are supposed to be immature** and put down other kids their age, right? That way they can make sure people aren't looking at **THEIR** human flaws, but someone else's.

We were merciless. These guys' sexuality was questioned, their appearance was made fun of, and they were outcasts from the "normal" group of guys. **Did anyone ever stick up for them?** None that I can remember, including me.

I don't know if I could have helped get the really obnoxious guys off of their backs, but I wish I would have tried. You see, I didn't realize these guys had been uniquely created by a loving God. By the time our final high-school years arrived, the teasing had finally stopped. **But it was too late.** These guys were so used to hearing rotten stuff about themselves . . . they acted as if they believed it. They were withdrawn, shy, and perhaps forever banished from believing the truth about their worth to God.

When my five-year reunion came around, my life had been changed by Jesus Christ. I looked for them to apologize and to let them know about the Creator I had met. No surprise, they weren't there.

There are classmates you walk by every day in the halls who suffer the same kind of abuse. **It takes a lot of risk,** but we believe you can make a significant difference in the life of perhaps one person who's been bombarded with lies by an insecure and immature crowd.

Stick up for them and try to stop the verbal assault. Tell them that they aren't worthless. Because if you're a true believer in Christ, you know how much worth they have. **Jesus shed His blood for them, just as He did for you.**

41. REFUSE to laugh at racial or off-color jokes.

And we're not just talking about in the locker room, on the field, or in the cafeteria. **You'll have plenty of opportunities** in the hallway, through notes being passed, and before class starts **to let others know you're not interested in taking part in this kind of talk.**

Get ORGANIZED.

Not just with your schoolwork, but with your *life*. You see, when you can get **YOU** organized, it'll naturally overflow to your schoolwork, your relationships, and your future. Want to know more? Read on . . . .

THE DISORGANIZED PERSON'S GUIDE TO GETTING ORGANIZED

If you know you have a bedroom **SOMEWHERE** *but you're having trouble finding it . . . there's help!*

Sometimes life is just too much, meaning: (1) You *do* too much, and (2) you *have* too much. That's why you often find yourself on the run from school to work to the library to Taco Bell to friends to the store to wherever all day long, only to come home to a room that looks as if it's been hit by several hurricanes.

And you can almost live with that, except for the times you run from school to work when you were supposed to run to the library, so you run from work to the library to Taco Bell when you were supposed to go to the store, so you run from Taco Bell to the store to a friend's when you were supposed to go back to work. **It just makes you want to go home and crawl into bed** . . . provided you can *find* your bed under those mountains of clothes.

What you need to do is **get organized.** Getting organized sounds tough, with all the stuff you have to wade through every day, but it really breaks down into two simple principles.

Organization Principle 1: Be in the right place at the right time.

The reason it's so hard to be in the right place at the right time is that there are so many right places to be in at the right times. It didn't used to be that way. In the old days, you could list your entire *year* on a sticky note:

A. Travel to Oregon by covered wagon.

B. Build a cabin out of materials gathered from the wilderness while fighting off angry bears.

C. Get some sleep.

Now, of course, you can jet to Oregon and fight off angry bears before lunch. Or you can call the angry bears before breakfast. Or you can fax them in the middle of the night and make 'em *really* angry. That's modern life. **We can do everything so fast it's hard to keep up with ourselves.**

Be careful about using that as an excuse for being late to school, though: "*Myself* was on time; it was *me* who was late!" (Probably won't earn you any points with your teacher, and it might get you detention.)

Organization Principle 2: Get into your room without being buried in a major avalanche.

While those old-time Oregon Trail people could fit everything they owned into a covered wagon and *still* have room for twenty-seven relatives, you can barely fit everything you own into New Hampshire. Where does it all come from? Well, you know where it comes from:

A. The mall—You *know* you don't need that cute T-shirt in all thirty colors, but you just can't help yourself. And you still have to figure out where you're going to put them all once you get home. Not to mention how you're going to *wear* them all in your lifetime.

B. Catalogs—Why you ordered nineteen varieties of oversized throw pillows is beyond you. And so is the door to your room, with all those pillows blocking your way just like the Rocky Mountains blocked those Oregon Trail folks.

C. Other people—Sure you wanted that inflatable kayak for your birthday, but the question now is: Do you punch a hole in the ceiling to dislodge it from your room, or just knock out a wall?

Actually, a safer way to deal with it would be to **get organized.**

So if you want to start being in the right place at the right time, and stop getting buried in unnecessary clothing slides, here are some suggestions.

Here's Help!

1. Get a planner. This is one of those calendar books people carry around to keep their schedules straight. Just make sure you use it only for keeping your schedule straight, instead of other things people use them for:

- Scrap paper storage unit
- Pizza tray
- Used-gum receptacle
- Cat chew toy
- Second base

The point is that it won't do you any good to get a planner unless (1) you **actually write down your appointments in it,** and (2) you actually **read what appointments you write down** in it. It's the second one I have trouble with. I write everything down just fine, but when I finally get around to cracking open my planner again, it's usually to say, "Hey, look what I didn't do yesterday!"

2. Don't overschedule yourself. The problem with having so much to do is that sometimes you can schedule yourself into doing two things (or more) at once. Which isn't easy, unless there are two of you. And it's a good thing there aren't, considering the trouble you have keeping track of just *one* of you.

So you have to be careful to do only what you can do, instead of what you *think* you can do. **Bit of a difference.** For instance, you may *think* you can go shopping and write your final term paper in forty minutes between work and dinner, but **reality** will tell you differently. It takes a *lot* longer than that to go shopping!

3. Keep only what you need. Be honest—you don't need a T-shirt in thirty colors. (Fifteen, maybe.) But even then you're saving yourself from storing fifteen items you didn't have room to store in the first place. So if you want your room to look more like a room and less like the county landfill, you may have to . . .

• Buy only the clothes you can actually wear throughout the year. (Changing outfits eleven times a day doesn't count.)

• Not buy shoes on the basis of "Someday I might own an outfit they may possibly go with."

• Not try to jam king-sized bedroom furniture into a pint-sized bedroom.

• Not keep everything you've ever collected since preschool for nostalgia's sake. Trust me, those Odor-Eaters from your third-grade gym shoes can go.

4. Don't overburden yourself. The trouble with having too much stuff is you always have to be *doing* something with all that stuff . . . like bulldozing a path to

your bed. Much better to have around only what you can actually wear, store, use, and so on—and to have it in places where you can actually find it. That's my problem. I know I have this certain item lying around *somewhere*, but I'll just need time to locate it. Say a few days.

That's bad organization. If you want to be in the right place at the right time, **you don't have time** to rummage around the house for three days looking for something you probably don't need anyway. Okay, maybe you *do* need those Odor-Eaters, but if you haven't changed them since third grade, it's probably time to buy new ones anyway.

This article by Philip Wiebe first appeared in Brio *magazine.*

Don't watch your FEET.

Think about it. The **confident** students are the ones who are looking at people, not at the floor. Trust us. **The floor will hold you up.** And it'll still be there whether you look at it or not. It's not gonna move. (Unless you're living in Southern California and experience earthquakes four or more times a year.)

So walk with your back straight and your head high. **LOOK** into the eyes of the people you pass. **Whether or not you feel confident, you'll appear confident.** And people will be drawn to you.

Develop great INTERPERSONAL relationships.

Be friendly with everyone, but select your close friends very carefully. Look for people who . . .

1. Share similar values. We're not suggesting you try to find a clone, but when you hang out with people who don't even understand or respect your values (let alone *share* them), it's tough to maintain your value system.

2. Share common interests. If Becci loves computers and you just want to play softball all the time, chances are you probably won't develop a deep friendship. Search for friends who like *some* of the same things *you* do, so you'll have fun experiencing them together. After all, isn't that one of the goals of friendship? To do things *together*?

3. Share themselves. If *you'll* strive to be an open and honest friend, chances are those around you will try to do the same. **NO ONE** enjoys hanging out with someone who simply agrees with everything he says. Look for friends who will challenge you and encourage you to think deeper.

Strive also to **share your insides** with your friends (and search for those who will return the favor). In other words, if something's bothering you, it won't do much good to keep it all bottled up inside. A good friend wants to hear your heart. Be willing to share it.

45} SIT UP straight.

Okay, so you've heard this one before. But do you know why this is important? **There's an actual reason!** Here are the facts—and a personal story:

Have you ever heard the phrase "As the twig is bent, so grows the tree"? What it means is that if a young sapling is consistently bent at a forty-five-degree angle when it's young, that's the way it will grow; it won't grow straight.

Did you know your bone structure is still taking shape? **It IS!** And the more your back is hunched in the wrong position, the more likely the curvature of the spine will end up just slightly off kilter.

That's what happened to me (Greg). I hunched over my desk with my hands on my chin all through grade school, junior high, and high school. Then . . . I did it for five years of college! **The result:** I now have a slight slouching posture. As I've gotten older, this has caused me to have neck and back problems. I have to see a chiropractor monthly (they ain't cheap), I can no longer sleep on my stomach (which isn't good for you anyway, but I did it), and I have trouble sleeping nights and sitting in one position for very long. **All because I didn't practice sitting up straight** during my growing-up years.

So the next time someone tells you to sit up straight, just smile and be thankful. That person is only trying to make sure your life isn't miserable when you grow up.

46 Bring your SUPPLIES to class.

Yeah, you know, **the essentials:** paper, pen, pencil, pocket-sized TV, textbooks, notebook, Coca-Cola. (Okay, you know we're only kidding about some of these things. Who needs a pencil *and* a pen, right? No, seriously, we're joking. Well, maybe we're *not* joking, but we *are* serious. No, really, **we're serious about our joking.**) Okay, no TVs, Walkmans, CD players, or food.

Even though they probably won't say it, those around you will get **real** tired **real** fast of you're always asking to borrow a sheet of paper. Or a pencil. Or a term paper. Get your **own stuff.** And bring it to class. You'll feel more prepared, which will result in better work. Really! (We wouldn't lie about a thing like this. We may *joke* about it, but we wouldn't lie. We're serious, remember?)

Learn to MANAGE your time well.

Ever wonder why **some kids never have any homework?**

It's probably because they've either bribed the teacher with a weekly delivery of their mom's chocolate Mississippi Mud Cake, or they've learned to manage their time well. (My guess, it's the time thing. Hey, I used to *be* a teacher . . . and well, I learned **NOT** to always eat what students gave me!)

Once in a while, your teacher will give you some free time toward the end of class. Even if it's only five or ten minutes, take advantage of it and start on your homework. **Try hard not to waste your time, rather take advantage of it.** Learn to make your time work for you so you won't have to work overtime.

Invite your YOUTH LEADER to lunch at school.

Many school districts allow you to have an occasional guest. As long as he checks in at the office, he can visit your school. **Why?**

First, **it will make it easier to invite your friends to youth group** if they've at least met the leader. All you have to do is introduce them and let the leader take it from there. What you don't want to do is put your friend on the spot. "Hey, Maryanne! I want to introduce you to Larry, the youth pastor at my church. Did I tell you we're having a lock-in this Friday night? Do you want to come?" Save the invites for later in case they have to say no. That way they don't embarrass themselves (or you).

Second, a school lunch is often **the best way to get thirty minutes of his time** so you can talk. No, it doesn't have to turn into a big counseling session, but it's tough to get to know someone by talking to him before and after Wednesday night meetings.

Go ahead, check with your school to see if it's possible, then **invite a youth leader to lunch.**

49 SMILE a lot.

People may wonder what your "problem" is, but that's okay.

If they knew the **Creator of the universe** and actually had Him in their hearts—they'd smile more often, too.

50} GUYS, respect the opposite sex.

Rude noises may seem natural to the guys you hang out with, but they certainly won't make a girl feel good about being around you. Be kind and polite! Girls are drawn to guys who learn to develop this side of their personality.

Are you walking out of the school building at the same time as Lisa? Open the door for her. Is Hannah's hair especially pretty today? Tell her. Did Melissa do a great job on her oral book report? Let her know. And **be genuine** about it. Girls are attracted to guys who make them feel good about themselves.

GIRLS, respect the opposite sex.

Every guy in the world likes to feel appreciated by the opposite sex. If Brad opens the door for you, thank him. Does Randy look nice today? Tell him. You've noticed that Doug's wearing a new shirt? Compliment him on it. **Help the opposite sex feel good about themselves.** And help them feel good about being around *you* by being a lady.

Other ways:

- Say something you heard about or saw in a sport he's in.
- **If you see him do a random act of kindness, comment on it.**
- If he's got high moral standards, encourage him to keep going strong.

Don't JUDGE people based on appearance.

You're going to come in contact with a lot of strange-looking people in your lifetime, many of them during your teenage years. Their hair color will be a shade of purple you don't care for; they'll have perhaps **ten too many earrings** in their ears; that tattoo will look just slightly satanic; their language will be a little "saltier" than yours; and perhaps their music will be a step below **dueling chainsaws.**

The natural reaction is either to stare, turn away in disgust, or say something uplifting to your friend such as, "Now I know why there's a hell."

The problem isn't with their appearance, it's with their heart. You see, some kids at school don't have a moral foundation for living. Either their parents haven't given them one, or they've rejected it. Their rebellious looks are usually just a cover for a hurting or seeking heart. Really! They want to be individuals, but they also want to be loved and accepted for who they are. Their appearance is the way they've learned to accomplish both goals.

It's tough to do, but **look beyond the rough exterior** and peek inside at the real person. More than likely, if Jesus were walking the earth today, these would be the types of people He'd hang out with. "It's not the healthy who need a doctor," He once said, "but the sick."

Exhibit school SPIRIT.

After all, you only go through high school once (well, *hopefully*), so make the most of these years. **Take pride in your school** and have a great time at pep rallies. Yell and scream as much as you can, support your teams, and try to join as many clubs and organizations as your schedule allows. In other words, **ENJOY YOURSELF!**

Befriend a HANDICAPPED person.

Most every school has someone in a wheelchair, a blind or deaf person, a guy or a girl who's a little "slower" than the rest. You may not realize it, but these are probably the loneliest people in school. Their circle of friends is small, and it's likely **everyone else just tries to avoid talking with them.**

Of course, there are some exceptions, but sadly, that's the way it is for most of these students.

The dilemma, of course, is that these kids aren't as popular as everyone else. And **hanging around with them could be hazardous to your own popularity.**

Boy, that last sentence sure was a hard one to write. The truth is tough to talk about, and no one would want to admit to being so shallow that she'd avoid a cripple because befriending him would drag her down the popularity ladder.

But it's true, isn't it?

Okay, this next challenge is only for the select few who are comfortable with themselves and who really want to make a difference in someone else's life: **Take the risk** and make a friend with someone whom life has seemingly shortchanged. It will probably be the most Christlike thing you do during your teenage years. And this we know: **God will reward you** in some way, at some time, when you least expect it.

Promise.

55 Be GRATEFUL for fire drills.

Hey, it really is important to know what to do in case of a disaster! And **it kind of breaks up the day, which is always nice . . . .** unless it's below freezing outside.

Just don't ever pull the fire alarm as a joke. It's against the law, and you'll end up with a **LOT** more to worry about than just making up homework for the class you missed!

People aren't looking at your ZITS.

Did you know that **WE** notice our imperfections **WAY** more than others do?

And did you know that those who do **POINT OUT** your imperfections are just trying to draw attention away from **THEIR** imperfections?

And further, did you know that **the coolest people** are those who keep their mouth closed and **don't point out imperfections in ANYONE**—even themselves?

What's the big deal about saying something about a zit or something that everyone already notices? It may get a laugh from other simple-minded morons, but it's not that funny. It's actually sad.

Sad because the person who says it hasn't learned the skill of accepting others (and himself) for who they are; and for whom **God made them** to be.

So the next time you're tempted to point out that someone has a volcano on her chin, fight the urge . . . because next week **it might be you.**

Wear COMFORTABLE clothes to school.

Too-tight jeans or skirts, itchy sweaters, shoes that are too small, and belts that don't fit will only make you uncomfortable during school. The result? You'll be less attentive during class. **Dress smart.** This includes wearing clean clothes that look and feel great on you. When you feel comfortable with what you're wearing, you naturally **feel better** about facing the day.

Don't joke around about AIDS.

It may *seem* like the disease of the future, but it's not. It's the disease of *right now.* Chances are, some of your friends will lose a loved one because of AIDS. Learn all you can about it. And don't write it off as simply a "gay disease." It's sweeping our country like an out-of-control brushfire. For more information, read Susie's story.

I'm SICK of AIDS!
I dare you to read this anyway.

Maybe, like me, you've heard all the AIDS stuff you can handle. You've been to the school assemblies. Seen the brochures. Listened to the special speakers. And **you're very tired of it.**

I was, too.

Until I met Nanteza. Her parents died of AIDS, so she was sent to live with her aunt. Her aunt died of AIDS, so she was sent to live with her grandmother. Her grandmother died of AIDS, so she was sent to live with *another* aunt. Twelve-year-old Nanteza is also HIV-positive, but she doesn't know it. Her aunt won't tell her.

NOW HOLD ON. Please don't skip this. Despite how it sounds, this is not a story about *everybody* getting AIDS, nor is it another hunger story about a bunch of "someones" you can't relate to. But it is about a few teens just like you. They may stand on a different continent and look a little different. But you're alike on the inside. Will you take some time to get to know them?

I gotta warn you, though. If you're not ready to step out of your comfort zone, stop right now—because **this isn't fiction; it's reality.**

But if you're willing to let God break your heart, and if you really care about others, then you and I are on the same wavelength. Read on.

It All Started When . . .

My friend Monica, from Compassion International, invited me to see the AIDS problem firsthand. So I went. To Uganda, Africa—where AIDS began. In fact, it's the most prominent place in the *world* right now for AIDS. And **it's not a "gay" thing;** homosexuality is practically unheard of over there. Rather, it's spread through sexual abuse, multipartner marriages, and unsanitary health practices.

• • • • •

Meet Nightie. She's fifteen years old and lives in a house made of mud and bamboo. Her mom died of AIDS at a time when a girl really *needs* her mother—at the beginning of her teen years. She has no one to question about her period, boys, her changing body, or her fears.

Even though she's wearing her school uniform, she had to miss classes today . . . . too much to do at home. You see, **her dad is dying of AIDS.** Her older brother, Vincent, would *love* to be in school right now, but he had to drop out when he was eleven to care first for his dying mom, and now his sick father.

I've just come from the nearby school and see Nightie and Vincent occupied outside with chores. I've heard about their dad and want to talk with him. Nightie invites me in, and I sit on the dirt floor.

"What's it like?" I say. Somehow they know I'm asking

about AIDS—about what it's like to have it. What it's like to die.

John (Vincent and Nightie's dad) is stretched out on the floor, his back propped against the wall. "My legs go numb," he says. "There are times I can't even move them. I'm dizzy a lot, and I've lost weight." At one time he weighed 175 pounds. Now he's down to 105. He has severe diarrhea and several other terrible symptoms of full-blown AIDS.

Nightie, sitting quietly next to Vincent, reaches out to her younger sister and pulls her close.

"What will happen when he's gone?" I ask.

Everyone is silent. **They don't KNOW what will happen.** Vincent tells me he tries to find odd jobs, but they're scarce. Nightie explains that sometimes she's able to bring leftover food home from school.

"We have *nothing*," Vincent says.

I learn that the neighbors of the village built them this mud house so they would at least have a roof over their heads. "But we don't even own the land it's on," Vincent explains.

Where will they go in a few months when Dad has died? **I already feel sick to my stomach,** so I don't even ask.

I stare at Vincent, who's trying to be strong for the others. He should be playing ball instead of having to worry about keeping a family alive. "How do you handle all this responsibility?" I ask.

Up to now, Vincent has been very involved in our conversation—acutely aware of all that's going on inside their mud home. But now, he quickly turns his head. He grabs the dirty T-shirt he's wearing and pulls it up to his face, smothering his eyes. His head begins to shake. Vincent is broken. Weeping.

I walk outside and begin crying. I look at my watch—it's a GUCCI. I glance down at my feet—NIKE Airs. I'm wearing a cool, bright orange T-shirt with "Nashville" splashed across the front and a Mickey Mouse cap. Suddenly it all seems so unfair.

Vincent lovingly picks up his dad, props him on the back of his bicycle, and pedals him across dirt roads to an AIDS clinic where he can receive medication for diarrhea and other problems.

I wipe my eyes and head down the dirt road toward the school. My thoughts carry their own conversation. *Orphans.* **It's just a matter of time before these kids will be orphans.** *At least Nightie is a sponsored Compassion child. She'll always go to school, have clothes, and be cared for.*

But the others. What will happen to them? They can't help it that AIDS has robbed them of a family!

●　●　●　●　●

This is Birabwa. She's 14 years old and—for one of the reasons I mentioned earlier—is HIV-positive. But she doesn't know it. She's missed a lot of school and doesn't understand why she can't get well. Her mom doesn't want to believe her daughter will soon have AIDS, so she hasn't told Birabwa that she has the virus.

When I meet her mom, I'm angry. "It says right here, on this physician's report, that Birabwa is HIV-positive."

"The report is wrong," she says. **"My daughter is not HIV-positive, and she will not get AIDS!"**

I want to scream. I want to shake her. I **WANT** to hug Birabwa and help her understand why she feels so sick all the time.

Instead, I leave and find Birabwa. "I understand you've been sick," I say. "What does it feel like?"

"It feels like worms are crawling around on the inside of me," she says. "I have real bad stomachaches. I get ugly skin rashes all over my body, and I have diarrhea all the time."

I change the subject. "How did you become a Christian?"

"I heard about Jesus from my Sunday school teacher. She talked on and on about how much He loves us. **It didn't take me long to realize how much I needed Him,** so I bowed my head and committed my life to Him."

I turn my head so she won't see my eyes fill with tears. *She's so happy,* I think. *Doesn't have a clue what's going on with her body, but she's so proud of her relationship with God.* **What a testimony!**

Since Birabwa loves music, I find a drum so she can sing and play for me. As I watch her eyes dance and hear her songs, I can't help but wonder how much longer she'll be able to do this. *She's so weak, they had to carry her over here,* I remind myself. *What does she have? A couple of years? A couple of months?*

• • • • •

Nassiwa is 14 years old and lives with an old peasant woman in the village. Why? Because she's an orphan. AIDS took her parents.

"How did it *feel,*" I say, "to bury your mom and be left all alone?"

"I can't even describe the emptiness," she says, "when I watched them toss dirt on top of my mom's grave and realized I'd been left to fend for myself. I'm lonely and angry. God is close, and He strengthens me, but I ache terribly for my mom and dad. I miss them so much I can't stand it at times!"

I feel the knot surfacing in my throat and know **I'm on the edge of tears again.** So I change the subject. I decide to tell her about North-American girls.

"Nassiwa, you have a few differences with teen girls in different parts of the world, but you also have a lot in common. For instance, many teen girls like to shop. What about you? Do you enjoy shopping?"

"I shop at the market for clothes and socks. If I had enough money, I'd like to buy a mattress someday. I have no bed."

I stop before she finds out that millions of North American girls spend *their* money on makeup, perfume, cassettes, and pizzas. (It seems totally incongruous.) "Anything specific you'd like to say to them?"

"I'd warn them about **AIDS. It's not a disaster waiting to happen; it's happened!** Follow God's plan for your lives and don't even *consider* a sexual relationship outside of marriage."

"In North America," I say, "teen girls often worry about their hair . . . and boys. What do *you* worry about, Nassiwa?"

"Hair?"

"Yeah."

"Hair???"

Her eyes are like saucers. She can't comprehend that people would worry about something so frivolous. I repeat my question. "What do *you* worry about, Nassiwa?"

"I worry about what will happen to me when the peasant woman I live with dies."

And the knot in my throat returns. This time I can't hide it. For the umpteenth time, my eyes swell with tears.

Why is it, Lord, that we're so concerned about how we **LOOK,** *when Nassiwa's concerned about how to* **SURVIVE?**

What Kind of Difference Can You Make?

If *you're* interested in changing a life forever, please consider sponsoring someone. For just $24 a month, Christian groups will enroll the child in school, give him or her supplies and a hot meal every day. From that, someone receives **HOPE.** Because by getting an education and by learning about a personal relationship with Christ, the person you help will have the strength not only to survive but to rise above poverty.

That's exactly what's happening with Kabula. He's a 12-year-old orphaned by AIDS who lives with his blind grandfather. The school he attended had to relocate because there were so many AIDS-related deaths.

When the school was being moved, Kabula and his grandfather misunderstood the school officials and thought it was shutting down. So when it reopened, he missed classes . . . . and no one knew where he was, since he didn't have an address.

But because he's a sponsored child, *someone* was sending in $24 a month to the school for his welfare—he had to be found.

The search party combed the area near the school, neighboring villages, and even bush country. **It took three months to find him,** but Kabula was finally located.

"Kabula! The school has moved. And since you're sponsored, your fees are paid. We want you to come back!" school officials told him.

"I was so happy!" Kabula says. "And fortunate. Just think: If someone wasn't sponsoring me, no one would have come looking for me."

"What did you do for three months, Kabula?" I ask.

"The men of the village forced me to dig ditches," he says. "For three long months, I just dug ditches."

Though Kabula doesn't have a mom or dad—and even though AIDS has changed his life forever—he has a chance at survival because someone cares enough to be his sponsor.

What about you? Do YOU care enough to do something about the havoc AIDS has wreaked on innocent lives? As Christians, Christ calls us to **make a difference. Will you?**

SUSIE'S SUGGESTIONS:

1. Check with your pastor to find out if your local church or denomination has a sponsorship program. You may want to plug into what your congregation is already doing.

2. **Sponsor someone . . . .** either with your family or by yourself.

3. Challenge your youth group to sponsor a child. I'll bet if all the teens in your group brought 50 cents each week, you'd easily have the amount needed each month.

4. I don't want simply to **TELL** you about Uganda and the people I met. I'd love to **SHOW** you. That's why Compassion International made a video

just for you that you can get **FREE!** Order your copy today (from the address listed under Compassion), and I'll meet you on screen!

Compassion International

P.O. Box 7000

Colorado Springs, CO 80933

1-800-336-7676

This article first appeared in the November 1994 issue of Brio *magazine.*

SURPRISE everyone!

Ask your teacher if you can provide hot chocolate or apple cider for the students in your class some chilly winter day.

Prepare it ahead of time in a large thermos and bring a stack of Styrofoam cups to class. **Everyone will love you for it!**

Be an ENCOURAGER.

Help your friends realize their talents. **Sometimes it takes a while for us to recognize what we really do well.** If one of your friends is always doodling, encourage him to consider creating some greeting cards. Publishers will pay good money for creative ideas—and imagine how good **YOU'D** feel helping someone begin an exciting career.

Or if Cassie enjoys poetry, encourage her to **develop that skill.** Is Bobby always reading comic books? Tell him he could create his own. A great place to look for publishers who are willing to pay for these ideas is *The Writer's Market.* This book is updated and republished every year, and can be purchased for approximately $20 from your local bookstore. It can also be located in the reference section of your library.

It lists every publisher in America (book, magazine, greeting card, video, poster), and will explain which publishers accept free-lance material and how much they pay.

When I (Susie) taught high-school creative writing, I introduced my students to this book at the beginning of every year. I surprised them by announcing, "For your first assignment, I'm going to teach you how to prepare something for publication. For a grade, you'll have to submit three things to a publisher. At that point, the assignment is over—whether you hear from them or not."

I stressed first that I wanted them to learn the *process* of getting something published. Then I continued, "At any point during the year, you can continue trying on your own to get something published. And if you actually *do* get something accepted for publication (from a publisher listed in *The Writer's Market*), you'll get **an automatic A** for the entire semester!"

Talk about excitement! Three students actually published that year. So **don't think you're too young** to accomplish anything. You and your friends have terrific ideas. Use them! Believe in yourself . . . and encourage your friends to do the same!

61. Live a life of INTEGRITY.

People will automatically **respect** you when they know you're **honorable** and **trustworthy.** Keep confidential those things that are told to you in confidence. Admit it when you're wrong, **be gentle to those around you,** and try to be at **peace** with everyone.

Be selective about the PARTIES you go to.

Wanting to meet and talk with the opposite sex is fine, but if you're going to a typical high-school party to do it, **you're not going to meet anyone worth getting to know** that well—especially (obviously) **if there is alcohol or drugs present.**

I (Greg) had a Christian friend in college who went to parties with other guys from the dorm **"just to socialize and be a witness for Christ."** Well, he didn't lead *anyone* to Christ, and I'm sure everyone wondered why he was there (since they knew he was a man of faith). Unless he went around to each individual at the party and explained to them why he was there, the chance of someone associating his presence at a party with the reason everyone else was there (to get drunk) was fairly high.

Yes, Jesus could go to parties and not care what the religious folks thought about Him. We doubt you can. The chance that someone will pass the word that you—a Christian—were at the kegger after the game just isn't worth the risk of damaging your testimony as a believer. Besides, those who go to parties usually aren't in any shape to discuss **eternal truths.**

Ever heard the saying "When life throws you LEMONS, make lemonade"?

Try it! When you're having a terrible day, stop and count your blessings. Write 'em down if you want. This is a great way to **turn negative thoughts into positive ones.** Go ahead. Try making a list right now.

Here are a few to get you started:

- I have a nice smile.

- People enjoy being my friend.

- I'm loyal.

- **I'm really good at** _____

- I like to laugh.

(You fill in the rest)

-

-

-

The next time you have a rotten day, come back to this list and add to it!

Pray at your FLAGPOLE.

On a specifically designated day every September (usually the third Wednesday), students all around the *world* gather around their flagpole for prayer before school. This event is called **"See You at the Pole."**

It's a great way to meet other Christian teens in your school while making an impact for Christ at the same time. Hey! **You could be a key person in helping to organize this event** for your entire school. T-shirts, friendship bracelets, and other promotional materials are available from the corporate office. Your youth leader probably knows all about it, so find out from him what the details are. If not, **call the SYATP hotline at:** (619) 592-9200.

STUDY at home in small chunks.

Have you ever had a **long** assignment that was going to take two weeks to do and you put it off until the last minute and had to work on it for six straight hours on the Saturday before it was due . . . and then you didn't get a very good grade anyway so you decided that studying was a waste of time and then your parents were mad at you and you felt bad because you were out of breath trying to read this **run-on** sentence?

We hate it when that happens!

The best way to study for tests is to do it in small chunks. Your body, your brain, and your fingers all need a break. We recommend you spend forty-five minutes studying, then take a fifteen-minute break. If you stick to this schedule, studying won't be so bad. Your reward for hard work will be time off.

The same goes for longer assignments. Ask your parents to help you **break down the work into bite-size chunks** so you can swallow them one at a time. (This is actually a great skill to learn before you get to college. Once you're able to do this, college homework will go *a lot* easier.) All you have to do is put yourself on a schedule where you're doing small sections of the work daily.

If you do this, **we guarantee you will get better grades.** If you don't, get a refund from your parents for the price of this book. (Hey, what could be more fair than that?)

66} Try not to constantly borrow MONEY from classmates.

There may be a *few* times when you'll **NEED** to grab a buck from an understanding friend.

But if you're always asking to bum a quarter from someone, you'll quickly gain the reputation of being a sponge, and when you really *do* need some change, people will be reluctant to give it to you.

MEET one new person at the beginning of every school year.

If you've ever moved to a new school, you know what a frightening experience it can be. And **when someone moves** into a new junior high or high school, **it can be terrifying!** A friendly face and a kind word can quickly turn their terror to peace.

Each September (and often at the beginning of each semester), new students will enter the doors of your school.

You have a choice.

Will you retreat into the safety of your own circle of friends and ignore new students, silently hoping someone else will befriend them?

Or will you take a risk?

Yes, it's risky to introduce yourself to someone new and attempt to get to know him. But it's worth it. You could form a lifetime friendship. You could be the one who introduces him to Christ. Or you could just make his day a little easier. All are good goals.

So this next September, **try to find one person who's new to your school** and befriend him. We dare you.

Talk your friends into trying a few random acts of KINDNESS.

Here are a few suggestions to get you started:

1. Give a box of doggie treats to your neighbor's pooch.

2. Let someone else be first in line at the grocery store.

3. **Say hi to someone you don't know** in your school hallway.

4. Smile at every single person you see for an entire day.

5. Surprise your mom by dusting and vacuuming the house.

6. Write an appreciation note to your pastor, youth leader, or teacher.

7. If you drive, give up your right-of-way and **let someone go in front of you.**

8. Sweep your neighbor's porch or driveway (or shovel the snow) as a special surprise.

9. Stick an "I love you" note in your dad's coat pocket, briefcase, or lunch bag so he'll find it sometime during the day while he's on the job.

10. **Empty all the trash** in your house.

11. Buy an inexpensive basket from the local hobby store, fill it with fun stuff (packaged microwave popcorn, granola bars, potpourri, cute pencils) and deliver it to an elderly adult from your church.

12. Make a thermos of hot chocolate and **get to school early.** Pour a cup (with marshmallows on top) and have it sitting on your teacher's desk before she arrives.

13. Find an old sock, stuff it with *another* old sock (or a rag), sew it closed, and give it to your neighbor's dog or cat as a special toy.

14. Make cupcakes for one of your classes at school. (Better ask the teacher first, though!)

15. Search through your closet and **donate the clothes you never wear** (and clothes that are too small for you) to Goodwill or the Salvation Army.

16. Offer to pick up used clothing from a few of your neighbors to donate to a local mission.

17. Get up early and clean a few car windows for friends or family members.

18. If you live in a city that uses tollgates, pay for the car behind you.

19. **Take your little brother or sister on a special outing** (to the park, the mall, the local planetarium, zoo, etc.)

20. Make dinner for your entire family. (Even if it's hot dogs or frozen dinners, your kindness will be appreciated!)

21. **Volunteer** to work in the nursery this Sunday at church.

22. Wash and wax your dad's car.

23. Stand outside the entrance of a busy store and hold the door open for people.

24. Have you watched something uplifting on TV recently? Write a letter of appreciation to the network.

25. **Give your mom a big hug and kiss.**

Don't stop here! You can probably think of hundreds *more* nice things to do for people.

This article by Susie Shellenberger first appeared in the December 1994 issue of Brio *magazine.*

Leave other people's LOCKERS alone.

Every once in a while you'll see an open locker in the hallway. Someone has forgotten to lock her lock, and now a lot of personal stuff is hanging out for the world to see.

Fight the urge to take a peek. In fact, **be a lifesaver and lock it** for them. In junior high, the cool thing was to know someone else's locker combination (usually someone of the opposite sex) so you could vandalize it (in order to get his or her attention, of course).

Well, that might seem funny—and it certainly will get you some attention—but fight the urge.

For once, **think about what Jesus would do.** Lock the lock.

Try to learn more from teachers and coaches than the OBVIOUS.

When I (Greg) played basketball in high school, my coach taught me a lesson that I never forgot.

"When you make a mistake on the court," he would tell us, "there are four things you need to do with it: **Recognize it, admit it, learn from it, and forget it.**

"If you can do all four in a span of a few seconds, you'll keep your head in the game and hopefully not make the same mistake again."

Those are not only great words to remember if you're an athlete, but they're almost biblical and could apply to any Christian!

Teachers and coaches have more to pass on to you than facts and plays. They're people who have learned a few things about life. Many of them are virtual wells of wisdom—even a few who aren't Christians.

Naturally, you should first discover whether the adults in your school have a Christian foundation (so you can know their advice is solid). But there are still things you can learn from non-Christians. **You can learn what NOT to do,** for example.

Some male teachers at school who aren't Christians spend too much time scoping out the babes. You can learn what a hormone-driven male jerk looks like by observing their behavior.

Other teachers know how to use their mouth as a weapon. They can virtually reduce a person to tears by making him look stupid in front of everyone else.

Learn from their insensitivity, and vow to never use your mouth in a way that would embarrass or hurt another.

The key is to watch and ask questions. Study people, and try not to be too proud to ask for the advice of another adult at school. Whether it's good or bad, you can still learn from it.

Your school may have a Campus Life club, Young Life club, or Fellowship of Christian Athletes (FCA) huddle group. CHECK IT OUT.

If you're a Christian in the public school, **you have two needs:**
1. To be around other Christians so you can learn, grow, and be encouraged by them.

2. To somehow and in some way **point those who don't know Christ in His direction** (notice we didn't say to "lead them to Christ"). If you're not trying to give away your faith, you're trying to keep it all for yourself. The Christian faith is not meant to be hoarded, it's meant to be shared.

Most cities throughout North America have one of these three "para-church" groups. **Their goal** is to help point teenagers toward a relationship with Christ. They aren't there to hold church, they simply want to **introduce non-Christians to the claims of Christ** in a nonjudgmental, nonpushy, and oftentimes **fun** way.

Most likely, your church is helping you meet need #1. Some even help with need #2. But if your church isn't, then one of these groups may be a great resource.

Find out if your city or school has one of these groups (check with your youth leader or the yellow pages), then get to know the leaders and **check out what they're doing.**

Some kids walking the halls were probably ABUSED.

No, we don't mean their parents make them do their homework or go to the relative's house on Thanksgiving, **we mean real abuse.**

Physical.

Verbal.

Sexual.

It's sickening to think that adults would ever do something like this to kids and teens, but it happens in every city every day. **Even a few churchgoing folks have abused their kids in some way.** More than likely, if you're in high school, the abuse against your friends has already stopped (though this isn't always the case). It probably happened when they were younger and more defenseless.

The **telltale signs** of abuse are too numerous and complex to go into here. We could say that if a girl is promiscuous, it might be because she was sexually abused in some way; or that if a guy can't make eye contact with adults, he was slapped around by someone, but that's not always the case.

The **important** thing to realize is that some odd behavior by friends or strangers at school is often a result of abuse—past or present. Don't just roll your eyes if someone you know is acting strange. Realize there may be reasons why people do what they do. **Try to show a little more compassion,** and don't be too quick to judge.

Don't SCHMOOZE teachers.

There are always a few classmates who have learned the art of getting on a teacher's good side. They ask questions just to make the teacher look good, they compliment the teacher in front of everyone else, they try to act as if they're buddies with them in the hallway—it can be so phony that **it's actually nauseating.**

Sure, **it's okay to be friendly** with teachers, and **it's certainly okay to display your knowledge** in class, but never intentionally try to schmooze teachers.

74 } SATURATE yourself with Scripture.

Thinking about God's promises throughout the day will help you **maintain a positive, godly mindset.** Consider copying some of your favorites on notecards and carrying them with you, or even try memorizing them!

Here are a few of *our* favorites:

"We are pressed on every side by troubles, but not crushed and broken. We are perplexed because we don't know why things happen as they do, but we don't give up and quit. **We are hunted down, but God never abandons us.** We get knocked down, but we get up again and keep going" (2 Corinthians 4:8–9).

"I pray that you will begin to understand how incredibly great his power is to help those who believe in him. It is that same mighty power that raised Christ from the dead" (Ephesians 1:19).

"Now glory be to God who by his mighty power at work within us is able to do far more than we would ever dare to ask or even dream of— **infinitely beyond** our highest prayers, desires, thoughts, or hopes" (Ephesians 3:20).

"Don't worry about anything; instead, pray about everything; tell God your needs and don't forget to thank him for his answers. If you do this you will experience **God's peace,** which **is far more wonderful than the**

human mind can understand. His peace will keep your thoughts and your hearts quiet and at rest as you trust in Christ Jesus" (Philippians 4:6–7).

"Don't let anyone think little of you because you are young. **Be their ideal;** let them follow the way you teach and live; be a pattern for them in your love, your faith, and your clean thoughts" (1 Timothy 4:12).

"Let him have all your worries and cares, for he is always thinking about you and watching everything that concerns you" (1 Peter 5:7).

"And he is able to keep you from slipping and falling away, and to bring you, sinless and perfect, into his glorious presence with **mighty shouts** of everlasting joy" (Jude 1:25).

75 Bring your BIBLE to school.

This is not only a great way to **be a silent witness,** but it can also come in handy when you've finished your assignment early and have a few minutes to spare before the end of class.

76 POPULAR KIDS don't always make good friends.

You'll notice there are four types of kids in junior high and high school. (And we're not talking belly buttons here.)

1. The "outties" who are happy and don't care about being an "innie."

2. The "outties" who are trying to be an "innie."

3. The "innies" who will do anything to stay there.

4. The "innies" who don't care if they're "innies," they're just being themselves.

We hate to put people in a box, but nearly every kid in your school will fit into one of these categories.

My (Greg) sophomore year in high school I had a great group of friends I hung around with. We did everything together, except get into trouble. **We were good guys,** but not popular— **we were outties.** Though most of us played one or two sports, we weren't the top jocks, so no one paid much attention to us, which was fine.

But **something happened to me** between my sophomore and junior year. I was progressing as an athlete and unconsciously decided **I wanted to be an innie**—more popular than I was. It probably had something to do with going out with better-looking girls (I was *not* a deep-thinking person). For me, that meant finding a new group of friends. I managed to do it. My old friends never said a word—they just let me go. I wish they hadn't. I got into low-level drug usage, tried to party (though I hated the taste of beer), and basically was

an "innie wannabe." Disgusting, I know, and I'm ashamed to admit it.

I exchanged peer groups, got new friends . . . and nearly screwed up my life. I wish I would have stayed with that old group of buddies. My new friends were okay, but I knew that if I didn't perform as an athlete, many of them wouldn't have bothered to look twice at me.

What I learned—albeit a bit late—was never to **TRY** to change from being an outtie to an innie. **Be content with who you are,** because that popular crowd is usually too busy trying to stay popular to worry about being real friends.

Learn to stand up for YOUR RIGHTS as a student.

What if a teacher asks you to do something that goes **AGAINST** your values? (And no, we're not talking about homework. We're talking about real morals here!) Do any of the following situations seem familiar? If so, **you have some rights** that you may not even be aware of! Keep reading . . . .

Classroom Battles

Your values are being **attacked.** What do you do?

The bell rings as you slip into your seat in English class. Perfect timing! Now, if only Mr. Milton would forget about that vocabulary test . . . .

Hey! He's not reaching for that smelly stack of tests at all! Instead, he's holding up the latest book by America's foremost creepmeister, R.L. Stine.

"I bought this book yesterday and stayed up all night reading it," says Mr. Milton, shuddering. "What a gloriously awful adventure. And I'm going to require you all to read it—even if you're squeamish. **You need to broaden your horizons.**"

Uh oh. You've heard about R.L. Stine's books. They're popular with kids at school, but they're loaded with words that would get you grounded for a year if you said them, plus sex, violence, and occultic evil.

"Um, Mr. Milton?" You timidly raise your hand. "Uh, isn't R.L. Stine, uh, a little *vulgar?* And I know he's gross. I don't think my parents would like—"

"It's no worse than what you hear in the school hallways and see at your local movie theater," Mr. Milton answers, the top of his nose rising slightly. "You're growing up now, students, and you ought to be able to handle something a little stronger than The Babysitters Club."

You feel your cheeks burn as you sink down into your desk. **Ouch!** You hear a few snickers, and someone whispers, "What a goodie goodie!"

What do you do?

A. You don't say another word. You'll read the book and let its garbage rumble around in your head. After all, the same garbage is in everyone else's brain, too.

B. You gather up your courage, walk over to Mr. Milton, and plant the tip of your finger right on the colorful blood-and-guts cover of Stine's latest book. "I refuse to read this," you say, spitting the words through your clenched teeth and summoning fire into your eyes. "And you can't make me. I'd flunk first!"

C. After class, you talk to Mr. Milton. You explain that you're not trying to get out of work, but you know you have the right not to be forced to read books that will fill your mind with profanity and garbage. You ask him to suggest another book, or if he resists, call a meeting with your parents to discuss your religious principles. You tell him **you're willing to learn,** but there are thousands of books that teach valuable lessons without resorting to gutter language or bombarding your mind with images of evil.

After English you go to lunch, and after lunch, **(groan!)** health class. Nurse Williams is wearing her usual no-nonsense white uniform and cap, and you notice that the guys have filed into their desks on the right while the girls are on the left. Nurse Williams waits until everyone is seated, then she places a small, sealed packet on each desk.

"Today we're learning about condoms," she says, smiling as she pulls a banana from her desk drawer. "You will each have the opportunity to examine one, and if you'd like, I'll demonstrate its use with this banana. And though you've heard this a thousand times on television and at the movies, I can't stress our motto enough: **Safe sex** means using a condom."

You stare in horror at the square white packet on your desk. **What do you do?**

A. You open it right away to show that you're sophisticated and worldly-wise. Just because you're a Christian doesn't mean you're not up-to-date on what's happening in the world.

B. You close your eyes and turn your head. No way! Never in a million years. You're not going to move from this chair or take another breath until Nurse Williams takes that thing away from you. In a minute, you might even faint and win a trip to the clinic to get out of this class.

C. You raise your hand. "Nurse Williams," you say sweetly, "what about the failure rate of condoms? And what about the statistics that say a lot of venereal diseases are still spread even when condoms are used? I think we need a new saying: **Safe sex means no sex until marriage.**" That's God's prescription for a happy life and a fulfilling marriage."

Your last class of the day is U.S. history. *Good*, you think. **What can be controversial about studying a bunch of dead people?** But as soon as Mr. Stone begins his lecture, your internal alarm starts buzzing again.

"Our founding fathers didn't want religion and the state to have anything to do with each other," Mr. Stone says as he peers at you from over his reading glasses. "They wanted to build a figurative **wall** between religion and government."

Mr. Stone puts down the book he is reading. "That's why we don't pray in our public schools," he says. "And that's why we can't allow Christian clubs on campus. It would constitute government sponsorship of religion."

What do you do?

A. You sink even lower into your seat and resolve never to wear a Christian shirt to school again. It's probably against the law.

B. You raise your hand and tell Mr. Stone he's wrong. You're not sure *why* he's wrong, but what he's saying sounds stupid, and you refuse to learn anything in his class.

C. You flip open a textbook on the U.S. Constitution. "Wait a minute, sir," you say, looking Mr. Stone in the eye. "It's true that the First Amendment prohibits Congress from establishing a state church. But it also says Americans are free to express their religious views. In many places on this campus, teachers or students are denying the truths of Christianity. But taking such a stand is just as much a religious expression as speaking in favor of them. **Why is one religious view allowed while another is silenced?"**

Mr. Stone clears his throat awkwardly, and you make a note to yourself to study history further so you can say more the next time an issue comes up.

What choices did—would—you make? If you haven't encountered these exact situations in your school, you may. And you basically have three options.

You can choose the A answers—do nothing and **go with the flow.** But if you're just "flowing," your Christian witness is likely to get mired in the muck.

Or you could choose the B options—get offended, **raise a ruckus** and make the teachers and school principal cringe every time you walk by. But what kind of testimony would you have?

Or you could choose C, studying a little bit harder and learning how to *reason* with others so you can **shine the light of God's wisdom.** Who knows? Maybe even your teachers will discover truth from what you say. Your classmates will pick up a lot, too. And you'll gain the reputation of being brave, smart, and dedicated to Christ. What could be better than that?!

(For a great book that's designed especially to answer tough questions that come up in school, pick up a book by Greg Johnson and Michael Ross called *Geek-Proof Your Faith*, Zondervan)

You're Not Alone

Remember the Old Testament prophet Daniel? His teacher (okay, it was really the king) tried to get *him* to do something that went against his convictions. **But Daniel took a stand.** And the Bible has recorded **lots of others** like Daniel's best friends Shadrach, Meshach, and Abednego—**who refused to compromise,** too.

So when you feel the heat, remember you're not alone and grab these three handles to help pull you through:

Fire up your faith. God can use the rough times to make you stronger—if you'll let Him. Try memorizing James 1:2–4. Then make a copy of **THIS** verse and tape it to the inside of your locker: "Trust the Lord; and remember that other Christians all around the world are going through these sufferings, too. After you have suffered a little while, our God, who is full of kindness through Christ, will give you his eternal glory. **He personally will come and pick you up, and set you firmly in place, and make you stronger than ever**" (1 Peter 5:9–10, emphasis mine).

Arm yourself with ammunition. Daniel politely refused the king's assignment but offered an alternative plan. (Read about it in Daniel 1.) You can, too. **The last thing** you want your teacher thinking is that you're trying simply to get out of work. To prevent that from happening, develop an alternative before approaching her.

What's a solid plan? One that doesn't skimp. Be willing to **do more** in your suggested assignment than what she's assigning in class. That's exactly what Daniel did. Then he asked the king to test him afterward, and he "tested" better than any of the other students!

If your teacher assigns a five-page written report on a book you feel is inappropriate, ask if you can do a seven-page report on a piece of classic literature.

Live the life! Even more than your homework, **your life is what's going to make the difference.** Daniel lived a godly life in the midst of a heathen court. (Sound like your school?) Others watched his actions and wanted what he had!

Same with **YOU.** If you want people to be attracted to God, then let Him shine through you! Are you always complaining about homework? If so, your teacher probably won't take you seriously when you complain about something that's worth talking about. In other words, don't be in the habit of crying "wolf."

And when you do disagree, **examine your motives.** Is it because you just don't like the assignment? Or does it really compromise your values? If you feel it's going to hinder your relationship with Christ, then it's time to speak up. And don't be afraid to involve your parents.

When you do speak up, talk in a gentle tone and with a smile on your face. **Give yourself frequent attitude checks.** Remember, your goal is to reflect Christ. It won't do any good to scream, "Hey! I'm a Christian, and I don't have to put up with this trash." Your teacher is going to think *Boy! Sure am glad* **I'M** *not a Christian.*

It's possible to win the battle but lose the war. So always keep *both* of

your ultimate goals in mind: (a) to become all God wants you to be, and (b) to make a positive impact on your teacher and the other students.

STUDENTS' BILL OF RIGHTS
ON A U.S. PUBLIC SCHOOL CAMPUS

I. You have the right of free speech and expression. In other words, **you can talk about your faith.** Just don't be rude and disrespectful to teachers and other students.

II. You have the right to identify your religious beliefs through signs and symbols. **You can wear religious jewelry, Christian shirts,** and you also have the right to talk about your religious beliefs on campus. Freedom of speech is a fundamental right that does not disappear when you step onto campus. Just don't interrupt or disrupt your teacher's class.

III. You have the right to distribute religious literature on campus. **You can give out Christian books,** tracts, brochures about your church's youth camp, or invitations to a prayer group as long as you don't disrupt school activities—such as your teacher's class—to do it.

IV. You have the right to pray on campus. **You may pray alone or with others** as long as you do not disrupt school activities or force others to join you. Graduation prayer is still permissible, if it is student initiated and student arranged.

V. You have the right to carry or study your Bible on campus. According to the Supreme Court, **only state-directed Bible reading is unconstitutional.** Research papers, essays, speeches, and creative projects on the Bible as part of the public-school curriculum are legal.

Looking for a research topic in American history? You could write a paper on "The Bible's Influence on the Founders." Or, for English class, how about an essay on "Biblical Themes in _____"? Just fill in the blank with *Moby Dick, The Scarlet Letter, Hamlet,* etc. If you're looking for a way to witness, you can even give a speech on "Why Jesus is Good for You" or do a science project illustrating the scientific truths found in the Bible.

VI. You have the same rights and privileges to meet with other religious students as do nonreligious student groups on campus. In other words, if the chess club can meet to play chess, **then your club can meet to study the Bible and pray.** These activities must be done before or after school hours.

VII. **You have the right to be exempt from activities and class content that contradict your religious beliefs.**

VIII. You have the right to learn about religious holidays (while on campus). **Music, art, literature, and drama with religious themes may be displayed and studied** as objects of cultural and religious heritage.

IX. **You have the right to meet with school officials.** The First Amendment forbids Congress from making any law that restricts your right to petition the government—in this case, school officials.

This article, by Angela E. Hunt, and the sidebar "You're Not Alone" by Susie Shellenberger, first appeared in the September 1994 issue of Brio *magazine.*